SO-BYK-409

The Golden Rules of Parenting

The Golden Rules of Parenting

FOR CHILDREN AND PARENTS OF ALL AGES

By Rita Boothby

CAPITAL
BOOKS, INC.
Sterling, Virginia

Copyright © 2001 by Rita Boothby

All rights reserved. No part of this book may be reproduced or utilized in any form or by any means, electronic or mechanical, including photocopying, recording, or by any information storage and retrieval system, without permission in writing from the publisher. Inquiries should be addressed to:

Capital Books, Inc.
P.O. Box 605
Sterling, Virginia 20172-0605

ISBN 1-892123-51-7 (alk. paper)

Library of Congress Cataloging-in-Publication Data
Boothby, Rita.
  The golden rules of parenting : for children and parents of all ages / by Rita Boothby.
    p. cm.
  ISBN 1-892123-51-7
    1. Parenting. 2. Child rearing. 3. Parent and child. I. Title.
  HQ755.8 .B6573 2001
  649'.1–dc21   2001017415

Printed in the United States of America on acid-free paper that meets the American National Standards Institute Z39-48 Standard.

First Edition

10 9 8 7 6 5 4 3 2 1

To Dr. Lois A. Vitt

Childhood playmate, cherished friend, and mentor.
Thank you for suggesting and shepherding my book.

CONTENTS

PREFACE

The golden rules of parenting are the rules created by loving parents

Parents doubt themselves too much. Reasonable self-questioning brings wisdom, but serious self-doubt is a paralyzer. As a family counselor I expected to meet and work with this problem, but I was surprised to find it so common outside the office—as widespread as dandelions and almost as hard to uproot. Mothers and fathers are criticized by friends, relatives, newspapers, books, radio, television, sometimes by their churches, and often by their children. This is a power drain. No wonder many parents confuse their own best judgment with "What will my neighbor (or someone else) think of me?" Mothers and fathers sometimes miss the simplest strategies because they're concerned about the targets painted on their backs.

A friend said to me, "But there are some parents out there with big problems." I certainly couldn't deny that. There are drug and alcohol addicts, abusers, etc., but those parents need professional help with their problems and their parenting. I'm speaking to mainstream parents who try hard but feel their power slipping away in a sea of disapproval. I hope to tempt them to go within to find their power, to change doubting to wise questions and self trust. I believe parents can sort out the overload of advice. They can, with their special knowing of themselves and their child, find strategies to match their own values. They can recall helpful things their parents did and decide which of those steps would fit their own children. They can practice listening to their own inner voice by insisting on time to do that: "This is important. I need to think about it and talk to you later." Best of all, parents can develop their imaginations. I've seen parents come up with good moves by answering the question, "If I were Jimmy, and having that problem, what might help me?"

Parent/child combinations are too individual for "one-size-fits-all" answers. The essays and small stories in this book are intended to highlight some solutions without insisting on them. Sometimes their messages actually conflict. In "Try A New True Thing" (Chapter 26), a solution hinges on a mom supporting a school's decision, but "Put your Mouth Where Your Money Is" (Chapter 25) invites challenging the system. The pieces I've written are meant to be judged by your own personal wisdom. Blanket rules are scarce. I do get pushy about newborns or gifting teens with cars, but I try to keep the ball mostly in your court.

The book is meant to send you love, hints, prayers, and especially respect, along with glimpses into corners you may have overlooked. Raising children is both singular and universal. Many parents gift themselves, their children, and the world with their labors. Many more have the creativity to do this if they will trust it. Parents who tap their own potential will invite their children to follow them along that path. When children trust you enough to let their possibilities peep out, you get to help them fashion probabilities they can someday choose among. That's exhilaration. It's a dream job with all the bennies except retirement.

—Rita Boothby

WITHOUT CRUST, BREAD WOULD NEVER END

The best minds in psychology agree that there are stages of human development. This is common wisdom as well. Parents know it instinctively, and knowing helps.

I was trying to be funny when I said this nonsense about bread to my children. I didn't really care much whether they ate crusts, and the birds needed those crusts anyway. I got blank stares, and eventually, the long-suffering, "Oh, Mom!" But it's true. Limits are useful. Children, adults and bread need them. Small children thrive on firmer limits because they can manage only a small percentage of their own behavior. They need adults to be responsible for the rest. If we try to make children responsible early, by frequent appeals to reason, very small children feel like failures, as if they *ought* to be able to do what we want. But limits, firmly and politely enforced by prevention or small consequences, tell children that parents are taking care of things, and they can enjoy their play life. Like the bread, they won't go too far.

The birthday-by-birthday plan is, of course, to transfer responsibility for more and more behaviors to the one doing them. However, ages and stages are not set in concrete. There are delays and retreats. Even an older child who is chugging along quite well, with reasoning slowly replacing authority, might need to run backward in time to that comfy old structure.

I remember a time it happened to me. I was ten years old and living in the bedroom that ate Chicago. It was a painful topic in our house. "I can't believe that child hasn't cleaned that room yet!" I *wanted* to clean it. I wanted to end my disgrace. I also had another reason—most of my girlfriends were neater than I was, and I wanted my room to look like their rooms. But something—I never figured out what—kept me from doing it. I sat amidst the junk on my bed, listening to my parents' exasperated voices discussing my messiness. I stared at a pile of unwashed blouses and wished with all my heart that my parents would stop talking about me or to me. I wanted them to open my door and cheerfully say, "Honey, you can come out again when it's done." During that odd little crisis, I must have needed to borrow a bit of their spine. My own was temporarily out of order.

It's a tough job. Another child might make Custer's Last Stand and start living in the bedroom. A parent's own special knowing of their child is the best way to figure out what will help. Lawmakers and judges spend whole careers trying to construct and enforce firm but reasonable limits. Parents have to do all that, plus fit it to the individual child! They have to become experts at trial and error. It reminds me of working with clay: roll it out, flatten it down, or firm it up. Find out if the limit is a real value or an excuse to have things our own way. Investigate, experiment, and pray until we find those limits that suit our values. Then we can fire them in the kiln and keep them forever to enrich our personal and spiritual lives.

> *Limits are like pitons;*
> *they are handholds to help us scale the cliff.*
> *We must study where to place them.*

MINIATURE WILL POWER

*The terrible twos can indeed be intimidating. The small
body now gets around quite well, the small mind does not.
If we can see that they are more like us than we thought,
it might help us create the strategies we'd like to try.*

The fragile bud of toddler will power doesn't blossom soon enough to suit adults. Everybody interacting with a toddler ought to think about his or her own will power. Very few adults snatch food from others or strangle the cat when angry—these behaviors get transferred to cruise control. But most adults struggle with a few will power issues like spending or speeding or eating. Even after years of polishing up the trim on our own will power, we usually win a few and lose a few. We need to remember that around toddlers.

Two people occur to me when I think about adult will power. One was a young woman who needed to finish a thesis. The other was a lawyer in his thirties spending his way to the cliff of bankruptcy. Both had plenty of will power in some areas, but both were about to hurt themselves. Friends and family were the temptation for the student. Most particularly, phone calls torpedoed her thesis: "I can't 'not answer' that ring," she said. She tried an answering machine, but answered it. She tried shorter conversations but kept talking. Finally, she realized she had to work on her thesis in the library and the computer center. For reasons she might or might not want to get into later, she simply couldn't resist the telephone. It had to be somewhere out of her reach.

The lawyer felt like he was a failure if he couldn't buy any gun he desired for his collection, or the newest car or boat. He came for help when he found himself selling his guns to other collectors to meet expenses. "I've become a retailer," he complained, "and not even a good retailer!" Although this man did work on how he allowed goods and money to steal his true identity, he needed a quicker strategy. The one he came up with was having an accountant he trusted dole out his money to him during this emergency. The lawyer saw that he couldn't resist his money, and he removed it temporarily from his environment.

So what's all this got to do with toddlers? It shows that even competent, achieving adults may need to have temptations put out of their reach. Maybe toddlers aren't so different from lawyers and grad students. Irresistible things may have to be put away.

It's exhausting but possible to keep moving babies away from objects or objects away from babies. It's also possible to turn homes into vast, empty plains, which is okay, but these parents will have to work super hard when visiting—they will have to shadow their toddlers to keep them welcome in the world. (Whether we're two or twenty, we know whether people want us around.) Most parents childproof some areas and keep others available for baby chasing. I also know a toddler who was able to learn "one finger touches," and got to touch many more objects. Make this "trying time" literal—try things you make up.

Cheerful, casual, confident, consistent—any or all these attitudes help. Harsh, angry tones scare toddlers and drive your intended lesson out of their minds. When the child stops crying, she'll probably go for the lamp again.

It's worth the monumental struggle to teach them, and it's worth experimenting with strategies, because children who win too many of these battles with parents are uneasy. I believe they feel much the same as we would if we asked the pilot of our 747 to let us take the wheel, and the guy actually stood up and left the cockpit. Small ones need to know that adults are in charge.

> *If the adult leaves the cockpit,*
> *there's no way the child can land that plane.*

ALLIGATORS, CROCODILES, AND LEO'S PAPA

The notion of making an impact on others is a great spur to learning. Sharings by tots are cause for delight. Correcting and expanding can wait until later.

A four-year old scampers up to tell Mom what he's found out about alligators. Pleased, she responds with information about crocodiles. The shutters slide down in his eyes. Both mother and child are disappointed without knowing why.

The late Dr. Leo Buscaglia, who wrote so compellingly about love, talked to an audience on PBS Television about his father. What he said explains why crocodiles should not automatically be connected to alligators. Leo recalled that his Papa required each little Buscaglia to bring a new fact to the dinner table each day. Their favorite sources were newspapers and the encyclopedia. Mr. Buscaglia had one stock reply to all offerings: "Huh! I didn't know that! Did you know that, Mama?" Because he was endlessly "impressed," they were endlessly "successful" in their pursuit of knowledge. Leo's Papa already knew at least one fact: success breeds success. Each little Buscaglia grew up to earn a doctorate.

I've noticed that comedians like to top each other's jokes, and fishermen like to outdo each other on the scales (pun intended), and this probably helps them, oils up their motivation. But, when it comes to children, I'd rather remember how musicians interact: They encourage each other to stand and solo on their own instruments, and then they applaud enthusiastically. They know that we all need our moments in the sun.

The boy who knew something about alligators was seeking to impress Mom. He viewed their talk as a glory moment, but she saw it as a teaching moment. In spite of good will on both sides, mother and son missed a minor boat. Single incidents never matter as much as the overall pattern of being a "receiver" of the fruits of a child's mental or physical labor.

We are already impressive figures to our children. We need to let ourselves be impressed by them.

COTE TALK

*Precious lessons disappear and die if delivered
in rude or unfriendly tones. Children,
especially, hunger for friendly voices along the path.*

Court-ordered counseling is never easy, and large groups of domestic violence offenders are about as tough as it gets. They don't arrive ready to hear about relationships, but sometimes talking about children can be an opening wedge. Most of the men have children, and each of them was a child. Understanding what children experience around adults (even around adults who aren't fighting) can lead people to see what's happening in their own families. I often ended a first session by describing a child's typical experience with adult speech as I've heard it both in and outside my work. Too much of that speech—and God bless the exceptions—fits into four corners of the same box: Criticism, Orders, Teasing, and Endless Instruction. The worst is criticism, especially when sarcasm is used to get laughs from listeners.

"Don't take my word for it," I told them. "Eavesdrop as you walk through this week and bring back anything you hear that's *not* COTE Talk." About half of the men did the homework and found that even nice people rarely say things to children that don't fit somewhere in the COTE box, with the exception of praise. A wonderful exception. We all need it so much. But we also need some talk that doesn't evaluate us at all, good or bad.

Several group members recalled how they had been spoken to in childhood and said they'd heard a lot of criticism, orders, teasing, and especially the endless instruction. Two men had tried talking non-COTE to their own children. Both said it was too hard to think of things to say. They were experiencing culture crush. It *is* hard to change the programming of our culture. There's tremendous pressure to conform, plus years of habit to overcome. Sometimes I still feel awkward when working for a better balance in speaking with children. But other times, I have so much fun! Children's faces tell you how rarely they encounter respectful, "no-rating" talk from adults.

So what's the big deal? Don't children need to be instructed, corrected and directed? Of course, but if we appeal to our own imaginations, we see immediately why we should balance our communication with real talk, friendly talk. Picture how we would feel if our bosses always spoke to us in COTE. What would we do if we couldn't quit that job? We'd feel rebellious, resentful, hostile and discouraged. We might even start acting out these feelings. Some of us might lose confidence, deciding that we must be awful if that's how we deserved to be treated. And the last thing any of us would do is go to that boss with any problems that came up. Instead, we'd ask our peers. Does this sound familiar? Crowds of children are reacting in precisely these ways. Adults and children are the same species.

Children can't quit their jobs. Kisses and hugs and I-love-you's are life giving, but even these essential loving acts can't bandage all the hurts of a day that consisted of ninety percent COTE Talk. Isn't it a marvel that most young ones can still plan and achieve even in the face of so much well-meant discouragement?

Real Talk is a foreign language worth learning. The cost of *not* learning is too cruel. We can begin by thinking back on adults we particularly liked when we were children. We can remember how they talked to us and what they said. Both images that come to my mind involve walking with an adult relative. One was telling me how she liked to make up stories. The other was telling me about a terrible storm near her home in Fredericksburg. Do we walk anywhere together these days? Maybe that's a piece of the answer—doing something together while we talk.

Real Talk has fewer questions and more talk about ourselves. Also, every comment need not be evaluating—if we are playing ball, instead of "Good catch!" every time, we can vary our speech with something like, "I love the thwack sound of the ball hitting the glove." (If it's true.) Or, we could tell a brief funny story about our own childhood ball-playing days.

Truth is big in Real Talk because secrets are never secret. Children tune in on us. For example, if we plan to share a board game, we need to choose one we enjoy. If we don't like games, we can tell the truth, "I'm not much into games but I'm willing to give it a try." What a wonderful lesson to model—that we are communal beings who can enjoy interaction with others even when we are not getting exactly what we want. Love is the language we are really learning when we balance COTE Talk with Real Talk.

> *A cote is supposed to be a shelter for lambs or doves.*

MONEY TALK

During a money crisis, it's hard to remember that children are small sponges, soaking up our words and feelings.

Early attitudes can steer decisions in later life, and tiny children absorb the attitudes of their parents. Remember Michael J. Fox as Alex in "Family Ties?" The writers gave us some good laughs by turning this truth on its head—they flashed back to Alex as a small child amazing his non-money-oriented family by adoring business and wanting his own portfolio. The plot line was funny, but in real life, parental feelings are contagious.

A young child who regularly hears parents argue about money, cry or get angry about it,or make predictions of failure, is a child already in money trouble. She's developing a picture of herself and her family as being upset about and lacking money. The feelings she experiences around this issue will be "scared" and "sad." If this keeps up,"not having money" may eventually become an identifying part of who she is, and without meaning to do so, she might behave in ways that keep it true.

So what do you do if money is tight? I've listened to women talk about hard times, and the semi-consensus is: Don't ride it or hide it. Don't make it the number-one topic in the house but, as situations arise, tell the short truth in need-to-know terms. Use time words: the idea of "temporary" needs to get through. "Right now, we can't afford to go to the ball game" or "Until we get a little more money saved up, we won't be eating out." Some women reported their own outlook improving as they learned to speak about the situation as temporary.

A confident manner can help a child step through a difficult event. Going to a thrift shop can be a treasure hunt or a shame-filled downer. A parent can make a conscious choice to model courage and cheer. And don't worry if the children get used to "second-hand"—they'll be sharing that idea with a lot of millionaires: Read "The Millionaire Next Door," by Stanley and Danko.

When money does get more plentiful, parents can turn the light of creativity toward wise use of it. If money is a faucet left running, children don't develop financial responsibility—they grow up expecting Mom or Dad to shell out forever. Parents whose behavior reflects righteous respect and pleasure in acquiring and using money are the models children need.

When the tide is low, be a buoy;
when the tide is high, be a lighthouse.

TO GIVE OR NOT TO GIVE?

*It's well known in psychology that inability
to delay gratification is a signal trait among
delinquents; less often mentioned is how the
ability to delay it can raise us up
as high as our dreams.*

Should we give children everything? Shall we make up for not getting things we longed for when we were small? Are we so sure we would go back and change that if we could? Those unfulfilled longings may have been invitations to become who we are today. "But I'll never forget not getting that sled!" Precisely. *Not* forgetting can plant a more important desire: success. If parents choose to deny only things a child doesn't care much about, how can that foster incentive?

Successful adults don't count on others to supply all their wants. The seeds for becoming a provider are planted early. It gets harder to instill this idea by the teen years, and it's a bear of a task with young adults. The parental balancing act—when to give and when to deny—is best done early. No rules, just parents following their best instincts, paying attention to the current status of the balance. Like ballet dancing, this requires both agility and grace, and grace means not rubbing it in or preaching when refusal is needed. A young child can learn to accept turndowns. Parents' tones and facial expressions determine whether a refusal feels like punishment or a chance to grow. Even if parents have a marvelous sense of balance, they'll never dance "Swan Lake" unless there is also grace.

Some parents believe that if they can afford something, there's no reason for refusal. If they have other creative ways to teach the provider role, their children may prosper. But many of us believe overabundance can smother incentive, and we seek clues and opportunities for teaching self-providing. People around us can be inspiring. My niece Janet is an impressive model for her children at stores. She picks up an item she desires and says, "I really like this, don't you? But it costs a lot. I better save up for it." My daughter Elaine and my niece Mary help their little sons save up for certain fun things. These children are "trying on" the feeling of supplying some of their own wants. Mary found a clever way around a small crisis when a scarce item was beyond her son's savings. She advanced the money after her son agreed to leave the toy on her closet shelf until he paid her back. Lay-away for tots! These incidents sound trivial, but they are the DNA of self-respect, the very stuff it's made of. A child given too little may believe she is undeserving; a child given everything suspects he'll be unable to provide so well for himself. In either case, we aren't looking at strong people who will make strong contributions to community and self.

Teens who don't contribute service to their family community and earn part of their goodies are in financial danger. There's very little time left to save them. It's like a wartime draft for parents of teens with no provider skills. These parents must serve and protect, be brave in the face of intimidating tears or anger. A big pitfall is getting dragged into yelling matches, where wisdom is scarce. A key move is to insist on talking later, when both sides are calmer. A second key is not giving up if we *do* get drawn into a hot argument—we're only human, and slipping is inevitable. The crucial step is to keep trying. Parents might keep from going AWOL by asking, "What happens when a person who is used to getting everything he or she wants decides that sex and drugs are appealing?" The answer to this question keeps many parents on active duty.

Another building block of the provider personality is charity. Giving money, goods, and service to needy people touches the hearts of children. The poor become real, and children see that hard times can touch good people. They also see their own good fortune. Until taught differently, small ones experience almost all of their wants as needs—charity shows them the difference. It nurtures both spirituality and self-sufficiency.

*Stand on the seesaw with one foot
on each side of center.
It's hard to do, but advisable.*

KIDS AND PARENTS SITTIN' IN A TREE K-I-S-S-I-N-G

In an Israeli study, mothers tried to identify their baby among three newborns solely by touch. Two-thirds of those mothers who had spent more than an hour with their babies could identify them by touch. Mothers with under an hour couldn't. Something so important is going on. *

If you're already up in this tree, skip ahead. Or stay and see how right you are. But if you're on the ground or a low branch, you may want to reconsider. Humans require touch. This is an accepted reality. Especially do little human beings require touch. In the 1800s, orphanages discovered that babies could actually die from lack of touch. Staff had to follow rules about holding and cuddling the babies.

Children need hugs and kisses from their mothers and fathers. (Fathers are closer to babies than they may think—in 1994, the touch study was repeated with dads, and it turns out that they, too, could recognize their infants by touch alone.)

Some adults say they don't have time for all that cuddly stuff. Exactly how busy is too busy for hugging? Some parents say, "They know I love them; I wouldn't work so hard for them if I didn't love them." Children don't know, just as spouses not touched don't know, that they are loved. The most frequent excuse I heard in therapy was, "My family isn't the kissy-huggy type—I'm not comfortable doing it." Is comfort a good reason to skip loving touch?

As usual, imagination (that magic drawing board of the spirit) will get you to the truth fastest—imagine using the comfort excuse in other situations: "Officer, I'm sorry about the seat belt, but I wasn't raised that way. We weren't a seat-belt-using kind of family. I can't help who I am—I'm just not comfortable doing it." By this time the policeman would probably be singing a chorus of "I can't stop fining you." Or try this one: "Mom, Dad, I know I didn't call to

---

*Kaitz, M., Lapidot, P., Bronner, R., and Eidelman, A.I. (1992). Parturient women can recognize their infants by touch. *Developmental Psychology* 28(1), 35–39.

say I'd be late, but I'm just not a phoning-home kind of guy; I'm not comfortable doing it."

How about a possible scene for your daughter: "Mrs. Hansen, I know the paper was due, but I'm not a homework kind of girl. It makes me uncomfortable." There ought to be a wise old saying: "Never make an excuse you wouldn't accept."

Consider setting an example for your children, teaching them that emotional comfort must take turns with duty—neither should stand eternally in the winner's circle. Inside us, there is the power to do things we don't feel comfortable doing. Choosing bravely is the challenge.

There are surprise benefits to learning to hug your kids. We already know how good loving touch is for our children, but we may have forgotten its power for good in ourselves. I've seen stiff parents, people who said they felt like phonies doing the hug routine, turn into more casual folks who didn't seem to recall they ever had a hard time embracing their children. What wonderful forgetting! May they never remember.

> *Not all beautiful deeds come naturally,*
> *but they can become natural.*

DIVORCE CHILD STYLE: TENDING TO HEART WOUNDS

Our most precious possession is reality. When a beloved parent says to a child, "Things won't change between us," things have already changed a lot. The child feels the painful truth and must discount either the parent or his own perceptions and feelings.

Why do people believe that children experience heartbreak in a mysteriously different fashion than adults do? There's no evidence that a child's broken heart is not a broken heart. To understand the feelings of a child struck by divorce, parents can recall their own early history, remembering the pain of any losses they experienced. If it was their parents' divorce, the fullness of the pain may be hard to reach; many young children bury it. But most of us can recall all too well the loss of passionate young love. We had no adult coping skills, no line of sight to the future. It was like lightning striking, even though we'd later see we had ignored signs. A child's first shock when told about divorce is also a lightning strike.

"Getting dumped" is a harsh phrase, but children feel like that when parents split, just as teens feel dumped when they lose the boyfriend or girlfriend they thought they would marry. Remember the hurt? Love was supposed to be forever. We thought we were good enough, smart enough, attractive enough, loveable enough. Then, in the blink of an eye, all those positive self-appraisals were called into question. The devastation varies according to the individual teen, but many go through floor-pacing, sweat-drenched anger; or meal-skipping, bath-skipping, school-skipping, sleep-deprived depression. These are aspects of mourning, and recalling them brings alive for parents a child's pain on learning of divorce.

Children *will* be devastated when they hear whatever words make them realize that Dad or Mom is leaving home. The depth of their hurt needs to become knowledge of our hearts, not just our brains. Even when children's pain interferes with adult plans for separating, even while parents are fighting their own pain, they can make time for holding and being with their children. Children need the physical presence of parents while they begin to absorb the loss. They need body contact.

Being intimately aware of a child's sorrow may also keep us from unintentionally twisting the knife. Think back to the distress of our own early losses, there were words we didn't want to hear, true or not true. These differ only slightly from what children don't want to hear. For instance, remember how we felt when friends or family tried to soothe us after a breakup by saying: "At least there's peace now instead of all that arguing." "You'll be better off in the long run." "He would have acted differently if he'd really loved you," or "I guess she found somebody she thinks is better. Girls are like that." We all remember how we felt when people harped on the faults of our lost love, discounting the relationship we treasured. Gruesome, wasn't it?

Communicating with a sad child is complex. Even a parent who properly understands the child's hurt is sometimes tempted to put a false sugar crust around some painful fact that the child must accept. A loving parent may say, "You aren't losing Daddy; you'll be seeing me every other weekend for sure, and sometimes more." The child *is* losing Daddy (or Mom, if that is the case.) Telling a child the opposite is crazy-making. If you don't believe it, think back—imagine a friend who said to you, in your grief, "It's not like you'll never see Chip. He'll still go to classes and be at all the games."

When self-evident truths are acknowledged, human beings, big or small, can begin the labor of turning adversity into strength rather than despair. A helpful parent tries to put together an accurate version of what will happen: "I am so sorry that you're going to see me only every other weekend. That must hurt you so bad. Whenever it feels like you can't stand it, tell me and tell Mom. We'll try hard to work out some more time together." Not perfect. Nothing can be. But it's true and respectful.

Continuing affection and loving touch are crucial, as is setting aside time to listen to the children without trying to convince them they don't feel what they feel. Understandably, this is hard for parents—they're human and in pain and want to push that pain away. I used to tell mothers in the crisis shelter—women too stressed to help their stressed children—when you don't have energy for anything else, just look up when the child enters the room and say his name. "Hi, Mike." Or simply stretch out your hand. It makes all the difference.

None of this is magic. Pain is pain. But when divorce is inevitable, loving adults can comfort, and they themselves need comfort, love, and courage to face the innumerable decisions and problems poised on the horizon. Friends, family and teachers may be helpful. A book that sparks solutions is *Helping Your Kids Cope with Divorce the Sand Castle Way,* by Gary Neuman. He understands the feelings and dilemmas children and parents face.

Sometimes a silver lining is just too heavy to carry.

RESPECTFULLY YOURS

*Very early on, computer experts coined the word
GIGO, "Garbage In, Garbage Out." GIGO is shorthand
for the fact that bad data input can't result in
good data output. This axiom is often true
in psychology, too. But fortunately, not always.*

"I might have listened to his problem if he'd come to me privately instead of challenging me in front of my _____." Fill in the blank: team, class, relatives, friends, etc. Coaches, teachers, and parents have all spoken these words, and they're right—respect does mean caring about how a person feels in public. When adults receive disrespect, they should enforce whatever rules are in place, but they should also ask themselves a question: "When I've had to correct this child, was I polite and, when possible, private?"

Real respect is tough to teach. We have to "be" it to receive it. Children obey the human instinct to imitate the behavior most common in the environment, especially the behavior of leaders. Modeling counts. Adults can earn and teach real respect by resisting clever words that get a giggle from brothers, sisters, classmates, or teammates. Adults can be firm and yet speak respectfully to a child. "Do unto others" is never truer.

Some adults get this point, but others make you want to weep. Everyone has heard an adult being brutally rude to a child and finish up by shrieking, "You're going to learn to respect me or wish you had!" Let's be careful out there. Fear is a substandard, cheap kind of respect that's closely related to loathing. It damages any relationship, and even though children are forgiving, fear will ultimately undermine love. What a big penalty to pay for thoughtless behavior that's often just a cultural hand-me-down from a rougher era! How immeasurably better it is for adults to study a child's misbehavior and experiment with solutions, preventions, and consequences that don't include grown-up belligerence or rudeness.

Other respect-killing behaviors occur daily in public. Nice parents, who aren't even angry, insult children while in the very act of trying to teach respect for others. "Billy, move! Stop daydreaming and get out of this man's way. You're blocking him." These scenes are so common that many people dispute that the words are unkind until asked if they would use the same words to a spouse or adult friend in that situation. In that frame, the difference is easy to see. A simple, "Billy, this man needs to get his cart past you," will connect Billy's attention to the man, rather than to himself and how embarrassed he feels. Perhaps it's too big a stretch to imagine that children who are constantly disrespected because they are literally or figuratively "in the way" might grow up to feel insulted when others get in their way. Like maybe on the highway?

This modeling thing is flattering but costly. Children honor us so much that they imitate us even when we're wrong. If children have listened for a dozen years to threats, insults, impatience, and witty remarks at their expense, do we need the CIA to calculate what "incoming" we should expect during the teen years?

*No need for a mirror in your pocket—
there's one playing on your living room rug.*

ALL ABOUT EMBARRASSMENT

What child wouldn't fight wildcats for an adult who treasures that child's dignity and tries to spare him embarrassment, even when he must be corrected?

Nature gives us embarrassment as a quick behavior changer. Human groups seem to delight in making and revising rules, and blushing is a short cut to learning these never-ending rules. We survive instead of being cast out of the group. Embarrassment is therefore a gift, but it needs a warning label: CAUTION: THIS IS A DO-IT-YOURSELF LEARNING KIT AND NOT TO BE USED TO CONTROL OTHERS.

Embarrassment works in a kindly way when we ourselves pick up signals that our behavior is out of line. When others embarrass us in order to control us, the cost/benefit analysis is grim for them. We flat out don't like people who do this to us and we remember it like elephants.

Some parents believe shaming tactics are a legitimate way to control a child, and some parents embarrass children carelessly without meaning to do it. In later years, when parents want to establish semi-mature communication, they find that their children are uncomfortable around them. Have you noticed how many teens treat parents like walking, talking embarrassments? Some of them may do this because they learned to associate the unpleasant feeling of embarrassment with their parents rather than with behaviors that parents wanted stopped. Humiliation tends to stay on the mind even longer than Windsong.

Parents shouldn't be afraid to correct children when others are present, but they might consider their strategy and start by intervening privately. Imagine a family party. Ten-year-old Jane looks up as Mom bends close and whispers, "Do you realize that you're kicking Tom's chair?" A rare transaction full of opportunity has just occurred. Although Jane, Mom, and certainly Tom are aware that Jane knows exactly what she is doing, Mom's behavior (1) invites a graceful escape, (2) implies that Jane will, of course, cooperate, now that she is "aware" of her behavior, and (3) allows Jane to view Mom as valuing Jane's feelings. That's a lot of work done by one little sentence! Cooperation is never a sure thing, but Mom has definitely increased her odds of success.

Adults embarrass children because embarrassment "works." That outward obedience is so desirable. Also, other adults praise us for a public "take-charge" attitude. And who has time to take a child aside? These reasons for resorting to shaming become powerful temptations. But children corrected with respectful and private firmness feel loyal to adults who protect their dignity, and some will try to curb their behavior. Being strict doesn't have to be public, until a child takes it public by defying your quietly shared instructions.

Experiment! Choose one behavior you won't correct in public. Take the child aside as you would an adult. Pretend the child is an adult, and speak the way a good boss would speak to you about something you should change. See what happens to the behavior.

Cats and humans like to lick their wounds in private.

A BEAR WHO LAYS BRICKS

Watching a fine parent is like gazing on a work of art.
Bear does it all: humor, discipline, sharing, love. He and
his son "shall have music wherever they go."

Some people are naturally skilled at making children feel useful and compe-tent. Bear the bricklayer is one of them. I met him and another bricklayer when they arrived early one morning to lay a path in my yard. They were friendly men, and one of them noticed the toys in my yard and spoke of his eight-year-old son, Tucker. He mentioned that he and his son share a passion for motorcy-cles, and he takes Tucker for rides on his bike. Bear (he had shared his nick-name) beamed as he spoke. His love was visible for all to see.

Naturally, I encouraged talk of children, my favorite topic, and Bear said that one day his son would have his own motorcycle. He described his conver-sation with Tucker about this:

"How old do you think a kid should be when he gets his first motorcycle?" he asked his son.

Tucker considered and said, "I think ten."

His Dad replied, "I don't agree."

"How old?" Tucker asked.

The amazing answer was, "I think eight."

Bear laughed at me. I suppose I looked as shocked as Tucker must have looked when his Dad made that strange statement.

"You can't really mean eight years old," I said, and he gave me his serious reasons: "My son will never be stranded in this desert on a bike he can't fix. He will know every piece of hardware in his bike, how to take care of it, and how to fix it if it breaks. He's going to build his bike." Bear figures he'll get parts this Christmas, and they'll get started after the first of the year.

The bricklayers came back the following Saturday to replace some cracked brick. This time, the second bricklayer was a short person with gold-ish-red hair. Bear introduced Tucker who helped him replace the bricks. I knew I was watching a boy who would never be stranded in the desert. It may take them years to build that bike, but a close relationship has already been built.

I believe Bears are necessary in our environment.

KALEIDOSCOPE THINKING

When peace of mind is splintered into pieces of mind as early as age three, four, and five, are we surprised when teachers complain about a deficit of attention?

No, I don't believe there's a conspiracy to scramble messages to and from our brains. But it's happening. No conspiracy is needed. It's a simple matter of constant kaleidoscopic demands for attention. Our children are becoming more and more distractible before they even reach school age.

The never-ending promos and ads that interrupt adult television made me wonder about children's shows. I taped a nice, nonviolent, half-hour preschool cartoon. The story was fine, friends helping friends. However, there were 18 minutes and 30 seconds of story and 11 minutes and 30 seconds of ads and promos. More worrisome than the time spent on ads was the way the time was broken up: there were 4 story segments and 21 persuasion segments. That's 25 changes of topic in 30 minutes. Almost one a minute. A truly ridiculous thought occurs—if teachers changed topics fifty times an hour, would our children learn better?

My admittedly untested opinion is that TV is fostering short attention spans in our youngest brains at a time when doctors are diagnosing a staggering number of children as having Attention Deficit Disorder. Too many children are on Ritalin. Where is the FCC? Where is the FDA? Together they might be able to stop the Ritalin Express. In the meantime, maybe we should tape cartoons and fast forward through the ads.

I recently heard that advertisements will soon be on school loudspeakers and in textbooks. I can't believe it! Will companies dare to distract students in the school building itself? Who knew Big Brother would turn out to be a salesman in the schools? In Macbeth, Shakespeare wrote, "Confusion now hath made his masterpiece." We could substitute "distraction" for "confusion" and bring that quote up to date.

Learning needs a workspace in the mind

TICKETS TO RIDE

*Certain behaviors, attitudes and even certain goals make
our children welcome almost anywhere both now and later.
We can help them with this.*

Limits, Attitudes, Purpose. (These capital letters spell lap—I didn't intend it, but I like it.) These three aspects of character are the indispensable tickets our little ones must have pinned to their sweaters so they can board that success train. With those three tickets they will survive derailments, delays, even the occasional accident.

The beautiful part is that we already know how to print those tickets. We can foster good behavior, good attitudes and a sense of purpose. Imagination will tell us how. We can pretend that we are behaving or experiencing exactly the same things as our child and ask ourselves what we would want a parent to do for us. Try it now and then. You'll see how much wiser you are than you ever suspected.

Parents can also brainstorm with buddies. Others sometimes dream up good strategies. BUT, there's a drawback to buddies. The two of you like each other and seek each other's good opinion. That's a filter and it can distort solutions. It's so easy to change your goal from helping the child to the goal of getting approval of yourself as a parent. The buddy has the same difficulty. So take those nuggets from friends or books or magazines, but never forget to run them through your imagination to refine them. Are they really gold? You know your child best. Be that child doing the misdeed or lacking a skill. Feel it, and ask yourself, "What do I need here?" Imagination is a gift, a drawing board where we can sketch out solutions for ourselves and for those God has placed in our trust.

*Imagination is a star within you,
and starshine enriches all it touches.*

LIMITS UNLIMITED

Children use consequences as temporary but necessary crutches until they grow stronger. If they could do without them, we'd be the first to know it. Tempered with kind enforcement, consequences make all the difference.

Some parents don't casually set and use consequences for young children. They prefer reasoning and don't know that they're asking their tots for advanced behavior. Most small children aren't ready to respond to reasoning, and if they do understand, it's very hard to obey. They often fall short and believe they're bad. Their parents want them to see the wisdom of the rules and use self-control. But that comes gradually, with many retreats and advances, as children get older.

Children test limits, and parents stop them. Both parties are doing what nature intends. In the beginning, it's enough if the child simply doesn't succeed in doing the forbidden x, y, or z he has set his heart on. As the child grows a bit older, families create consequences. But in some families, when it's time to apply those consequences, the adults plead with the child for good behavior and re-explain their reasons. These parents sound desperate to avoid using those consequences. How puzzling. Aren't they the right ones? If they're too harsh to use, they should be quickly changed. Kids are entitled to those consequences, and they need to be free from all that parental entreaty that makes them feel like bad children.

Instead of consequences, however, many children get the ultimate punishment. They see faces that are exasperated or disgusted; they hear tones of anger and disappointment. These are the beginning seeds of self-dislike which can become self-loathing. There's no bigger block to future success. Avoiding this outcome is worth lots of practice at using consequences.

Quick enforcement is key with young children. When unwanted behavior occurs, deliver the consequence you've chosen to fit your child. If that means going home, stand up and start gathering. If it's no cookie baking, announce it immediately. Behaviorists know that when even a short time elapses between act and consequence, the small child will connect the consequence to his most recent bit of behavior—which was probably ignoring your pleas to stop. In the child's mind it then becomes a game of avoiding the consequence by guessing when to stop ignoring you. Another strategy a parent may choose is prevention: If little Shirley gets a gleam in her eye and heads for Tommy's new wagon with a shovel, stop her. Confiscate the shovel, and say something simple like, "I'm helping Tommy. His wagon has to be safe."

Delay in correcting lets our annoyance grow and makes it nearly impossible to speak with the cheerful firmness that allows a child to concentrate on his deed instead of on the parent. "We have to leave the pool now because you pinched, but we'll try again tomorrow. I bet you can swim tomorrow without pinching anybody." The sad wail you hear won't really hurt anyone, especially the child. The tears are for lost fun, not lost love, because apparently you still like him even while you're doing this awful pool leaving thing. Strict measures don't violate love. Mean faces and loud angry voices do that. They "work" because they're scary, but the good behavior of a frightened child is likely to be an animal instinct rather than a sign of values taking root in the soul.

Often, a naturally occurring consequence helps parents cope. If it isn't harmful, all the parent has to do is let it happen. If the cat hides behind the couch, for heaven's sake don't move the couch. Explain that kitty is protecting her tail, and it might be a while before he can play with her again.

Logical or "matching" consequences can be fruitful. If a four-year-old throws food, perhaps she can clean it up, (with your help) and also do some other small task for the family so that you can end on a positive note: "We're happy you did that for us." When behavior takes away from family harmony, it's always nice to put back more than you took.

When children are small, parents set the consequences. As children get older, they can participate in the process—sometimes brilliantly. Today three children outdid both their mom and me. The mom phoned about a consequence that sounded fine, but later called back to say that the three children had come up with a goodie. Two had hit the third child, and they all decided that the one who had been hit would choose the after-dinner cartoon tape, usually hotly contested. Works for me. Even if mom has to enforce it. There's a nice little positive twist to their idea. And whoever forgets a self-designed penalty?

It's understood that parents can't constantly be cheerful and friendly. At least I never met one, including me, who could. But part of the time will do. Children are profoundly forgiving, and I believe they'll flourish if their busy parents discipline in a friendly, creative, non-blaming manner even part of the time. It's quite a gift, even to a child who refuses to see it that way. Both parties benefit because the child doesn't have to feel lousy—she simply has to pay a reasonable price to get straight with her family community.

Hurrah for brave, friendly, and experimental parents! They tap their unlimited potential.

REWARD

*Sometimes children obey the rules,
or work hard to get rid of a bad habit,
or act patiently with a bratty sibling.*

Parents decide on rewards as well as consequences. They know the kind of reward each of their children likes. They use a mix of emotional rewards, like valuing or praising, as well as more tangible rewards.

Occasionally the choices of teachers or other parents inspire us. At a time when I wanted my children to invest more effort in schoolwork, their school began giving them smile cards for meeting goals. My kids liked them, and I didn't want the shine to wear off too soon. I wondered what I could piggyback on the cards. I decided that the thing children wanted most but had least of was power. We called the cards power cards, and they were good for fifteen minutes off bedtime, or dessert before dinner, or other small opportunities to exercise power. We had to renegotiate to establish only one card per day. I hadn't realized what a great motivator power was going to be.

This is one of the fun parts of the job.

BEACH BOYS

Perfect fairness is, like the unicorn, a fantasy. Reasons like safety or the good of the family may at times outrank fairness. Children rarely understand this but nevertheless live through it and benefit.

Sometimes you have to make something happen. When the stakes are high, you can't play around. I had a brother-in-law who knew this. Maybe the Navy taught him to take action, and there's no doubt that actions speak louder than nagging.

John and Margie had six boys, including a toddler and a baby. A favorite summer plan was frying chicken for a picnic at a Chesapeake beach. "Limits" are quite literal around water, and the rule was clear: no contact with water until the playpen and picnic coolers were set up in the shade. After that, a parent would be free to take the children into the water. On one such trip, the impatient boys danced a bit too near the water and soon, one was wading ankle deep. John saw this but said nothing. Both parents had said it all before. Instead, John and Margie began repacking drinks, folding the stroller, and facing up to a long drive home with crying children. Easy? Good parents often find life not so easy. It was unfair to the obedient children, but John and Margie decided that leaving was fairer than a possible future drowning. It was also fairer than two hard-working parents unable to enjoy peace of mind on outings. Sometimes you have to draw straws to see who gets the fairness. In this case, it was clearly more important that a potential drowner and the parents get the fairness, even at the expense of some well-behaved beach boys.

The genius touch was letting the lesson stand alone. The parents didn't have to lecture beyond stating the facts. What they did said it all. When parents take a dramatic stand, they benefit hugely by staying polite about it. Unkind words permit the disobedient child to cast the parent as the villain. The offender's disappointment converts to resentment, and he takes himself off the hook by being angry with you instead of dissatisfied with what he chose to do. How powerful to say, "Yes, it is really sad. I wish we could be swimming with you (or at the movie, etc.) right now." Certainly true! And, it leaves the child a clear line of sight to his own misbehavior. Do you think any of those beach boys broke the water rules again?

Courage, truth and good cheer—a magic potion for families.

ON PURPOSE

My high school newspaper was called The Questor, a good statement about what all of us are up to. Conditions favor or hinder our quest for purpose.

Let's live our lives on purpose and help our children do that, too. Even small children need to experience the happiness of being valuable in their family by giving as well as receiving. As children grow, they need to imagine careers and begin to set small goals of service to the family. Without the grounding of appreciation from their family community, it's hard for them to foresee themselves as useful and valuable to the larger community. Purpose seeking starts early in life.

Children feel valued for their efforts when they know their work benefits you. A little child needs to know that you enjoy sitting in that room he dusted. A teen needs to hear how happy you are that you can plan your barbecue now that she's cut the lawn so attractively. Children need to hear that your freedom to play a game or help with a project flows from the work they do. Tell them so. Watch their reactions. You'll see that they'd rather be valued than praised— praise is good, but it will never match being valued. When parents become aware of this, they get creative about expressing appreciation.

Some families naturally encourage the seeking of purpose, but a few do confuse children about it. Some tell the child he is the purpose of their life. Raising children well is indeed a noble purpose, but hearing "You are the purpose of my life" can create a burden for the child. Being someone's purpose is so different from seeking purpose. It's passive. No matter how many learning activities fill a child's life, nothing is really happening unless the child feels free to think about a separate, personal future, a vision of herself moving into the world. Accomplishments begin in our imaginations, and children must imagine beyond the family. They are on loan to us, and there's a due date.

Another way to cast a shadow across purpose is to confuse it with self-importance. This happens when a child becomes the centrifugal center around which the family is pulled, and no one else seems to count. Understandably, such a child develops no idea of earning recognition. He sees that it's bestowed, not earned. One simple fix is to share importance among all members of a family. It's a turn taking thing, and turns needn't be equal or fair; they just have to exist. "I always come first" won't serve happiness. Future spouses and bosses seldom indulge "me firsters" for very long.

Unreasonable commitments also hinder a search for purpose. Overly busy children lose golden chances to explore a range of skills. Ironically, such children may also feel they don't really matter to the family because they are "excused" (deprived of is more accurate) from doing anything productive within the family. Their triumphs and failures occur away from home. They don't get to feel competent and valuable to their families by packing the lunches, and bathing pets, making fudge or playing games at the kitchen table.

Exploring skills is slipping quietly out of fashion. If a child has invested two years in swimming, all the pressure is to improve even more at swimming—rather than trying piano, or chess, or even a different sport. Build models? Rehab a bike? No time. Some public and private schools have developed big egos and don't want children to dabble with discovery. They want pupils to keep honing particular skills so that the school can win sports trophies or academic awards. A parent might want to weigh carefully the advantages of any activity that requires four or five practices a week and possibly also a camp where your child can learn to outdo other children at the chosen activity. The word kidnapping comes to mind. Notice that constantly empty place at the table.

There are encouraging blips on the radar screen, such as city recreation programs, local Ys, and boys and girls clubs, as well as church teams, clubs and choirs. These groups give children a chance to explore a variety of activities. Some groups even offer sports teams with alternative attitudes toward winning. Coaches are trained to emphasize enjoyment of participation and improvement of skills in a variety of sports and activities. And players of all skill levels share playing time. Winning isn't the total point. In much the same way, good grades and money aren't the total point of learning—they are pleasant byproducts of enjoying the pursuit of a purpose.

I have a fantasy in which some of the better school athletes abandon win-crazy coaches and join small teams to have some fun. Then those coaches would have to . . . Oh, never mind. Just scope out your community to learn what kinds of things are happening there. It could help your child discover what she will someday contribute to her community.

> *To be useful in the family called Humanity
> is a longing in our hearts.*

MONEY IS THE ROOT OF ALL OPPORTUNITY

Money, service, and purpose should fit together neatly like pieces of a jigsaw puzzle. This isn't easy. There are too many negative myths about money.

Does this title sound right to you? If so, you're not contaminated by the myth of money as evil. You probably buy what's attractive or useful and leave the rest alone, balance your investments, and provide reasonably for the future, all without guilt. And some of your money is likely to circulate in the form of charity. If you believe money is opportunity, you probably manage it well and accumulate wisely, even if you are underpaid. Your children are so lucky. They breathe in your good attitudes.

Money itself is an agreement among humans about what they value. If people stopped liking gold and diamonds, that changed attitude would make them worthless. We have a word for profitable items that don't last so well: fads. (Please let tongue jewelry be the next to go.) Negative attitudes are truly destructive on Wall Street. If investors decide that a stock is shaky, it drops like a stone, even if the investors are dead wrong about the company. Our thoughts about money are more powerful than the actual tangible assets! It's what we *think* that creates value.

What this "powerful thinking" means to parents is that children will pick up our good or bad attitudes about money and other issues, and they often ignore our intentional teaching unless it matches up. Our true thinking creates values in our children. On-the-spot reactions to money situations speak volumes. For example, if we take vacations we can't afford and run up bills at many stores and then avoid the telephone and the mail, children will see money as a grab-and-run game we play with other people in the community. Impatience, fear, and avoidance will be money attitudes they'll have to overcome. They won't see the beautiful truth—that money represents our labors, our gifts to our community family, our purpose. It certainly should not be an adversarial game we play with our community.

Purpose is further confused by another powerful myth: Humanitarian careers deserve low salaries because money (filthy lucre?) will attract those without a true motive to help others—as if you can't mix money and goodness.

All venture ministers in some way to the needs of others. And, if you can't mix goodness and money, where does that leave charity? Wow! Our funny ideas about money make it tough to send children clear messages about the necessary blend of money, purpose, and service. We have to stop hitting these notes one at a time—together, they make a beautiful chord.

Money and "goods" are the heartblood of both commerce and charity. Circulation is celebration.

MAKING ALLOWANCES

So many allowance strategies work well if the parent likes the system and enjoys administering it. The mechanics seem less important than cooperation along the way.

Parents who believe in allowances often disagree on the mechanics of paying children. Different camps can make seemingly opposing ideas work well. This is puzzling, until you notice that those who succeed give time and attention to running their system and feel confident about it. They seem to know their own kids and what will work with them.

Some parents even devise different systems for different kids in the same family: "I pay the others once a week, but I divide up Jeremy's money and pay him three times." This surprised me because Jeremy was oldest. I wondered aloud if he spent it all immediately. His mom said, "Not always. Maybe he would . . . No, I think he just likes to get something more often." Now, that's nice. In her family, not only can you be different, you don't have to explain why.

Should chores be tied to allowances? The Nevers and the Always parents are quite clear on this. The Nevers say that children can't possibly develop a sense of duty to family if they are paid for chores; the Always parents feel that incentive to earn will not develop unless pay for work exists in the family. A third group, the Blenders, seems at first glance to have it all. They divide chores into categories of "for pay" and "for duty." But the Never and Always claim this would lead to endless confusion and bickering in their houses. In general, families were satisfied with their own arrangement if not their neighbor's.

Charity, on the other hand, was an area of agreement. Most parents believe children should save a small part of their money for giving either through their church or to other charities. Several reported that their children were touched by ads about children who need food or clothes. One family collects toys for needy children. In that family, a child who wants a new toy must select one to give away. Encouraging a child's natural compassion benefits all.

If you're looking for specific strategies on allowances, I know of two books well worth exploring: Janet Bodnar's *Money-Smart Kids*, and Neal Godfrey's (with Tad Richards) *A Penny Saved*. Even if you don't find the idea you want, these books offer so many ideas that they'll spark your creativity, and you'll think up one for yourself.

Whatever you decide to do about allowances, be light of heart with it. It's learning, which implies that one did not know it before. Children, especially young ones, are usually willing to accept your views, even about how much money they receive. It helps to be supportive when a child blows it. Tell him not to worry; there will be new chances, and you know he'll become skillful at managing his money.

> *Children are newcomers to the world of money. Make allowance for that.*

AFTER THE LEMONADE STAND

*When two events are similar and yet we react very
differently to them, it's a big clue.
A button we didn't know we had got pushed.
Do we really encourage earning money?*

We definitely want our children to be enterprising, to work, to earn money. We reward attempts in this direction. Really? Is that what we do? Maybe we should sit on a rock like Winnie the Pooh and think, think, think.

We could take a hint from Junior Achievement, a program that helps young people experience entrepreneurial fun. The important word here is fun. JA's biggest benefit might be correcting somber, serious attitudes toward making money.

Those parents who do have downer attitudes about money usually don't realize it. What I've noticed is that a child's business venture seems exciting to parents the first time only. We ooh and aah over the lemonade stand and take snapshots for the album, but then it's all over. The next time a child wants to set up a moneymaking venture, parents usually sound like farmers forecasting poor crops. Take odds that our first words will be warnings about pitfalls. (See why people grow up afraid of money?) Our next words will be about how proud we are that our child is willing to do "all that hard work that never hurt anybody." (See why people grow up unaware that making money is fun?) Zap. You can almost feel the frozen ground getting ready to spit out the bitter harvest!

A little contrast, please. Think how we act when our children set out to play baseball or take dancing lessons or cheerlead, learn an instrument, play chess or get a library card. Almost any non-moneymaking activity will light our fire. Our eyes shine, and we start budgeting some of OUR time and OUR money. We create a "joint venture," picking up that batting glove or piece of sheet music on the way home. And our forecasts are sunny. "Wow, I had so much fun the year I was on the basketball team," or "You can't beat the feeling of making music together in a group." We are willing to arrange rides, and we want to hear any details the child is willing to share. No one ever says, "This baseball thing is your responsibility. It's up to you to figure out how to get there." They might, wisely, require the child to earn part of the money spent on equipment, but few parents would ever tell the child, "Don't expect me to get involved—this is your project."

Now that I'm wise to my old attitude, I don't believe making money has to be treated differently than other activities. Why not buy a shiny little cash box or a pad of receipts as a celebration present? An attractive book for notes on customers is instruction without talking—always a worthy goal. Why not mention at once some fun we had on a job? Why don't we offer time, say, setting up a simple spreadsheet with our son or daughter? Why not put aside a special notebook for the phone calls we volunteer to take when the child is not at home? We need to do something (almost anything) to show that we're excited about this new idea. Pitfall talk can be postponed and talked about casually as a natural part of what "we" deal with in business, not any more dire than errors in baseball or false notes in music. Is there a living parent who would immediately mention errors or sour notes when a child expressed interest in baseball or music?

We've been brainwashed. Those "filthy lucre" attitudes are lurking down deep. We may believe that there's something unattractive about wanting money. But we needn't be horrified that a small portion of our gray matter has been rinsed and starched. We can allow for it, disregard our feelings of doom and get creative. We can lighten up and have some giggles. If our pride and joy is planning a dog walking business, we can buy those wonderful poop-scoop bags and say, "When you're a grown-up rich woman, you can tell people your very first backer fronted you a case of Poopee Scoopees!"

Sometimes, work is fun or funny; almost always, it makes you nicely tired.

CAREER PATH/OLOGY

Where do careers come from? They come from pictures in the mind. Where do the pictures come from? Only the future grown-up can put the pictures there, but others can encourage it.

Even though children will grow up, they are seldom seen as future teachers, mechanics, lawyers, or business people, and almost never as future rich people, unless parents dream of stardom in sports or arts. In late high school, after blocking off some good career routes, too many students look for the first time at the future. No one has treated them as future grown-ups, and they're uncomfortable with this swiftly approaching concept. It seems dim and vague and difficult. To make matters worse, a haze of hormones may force hasty decisions.

Chances are that the high school will be too big to help teens clear paths they blocked earlier. When you're handling thousands of people at the most volatile time of their lives, it's tough to keep early poor choices from continuing to damage academic success. The gifted will do well, and if the school has specially trained staff to help them, the gifted may be spectacular. A second group will also do well—those inspired by an inner, unexplainable fire. A third group does well, too—those whose parents and/or teachers have acted early, knowing children need goals, and they need them before high school. Only God can put your children in the first two groups, but you can put them in the third.

This involves parents' free time and could mean sacrificing some usual recreations in favor of exploratory outings. Children also need to engage in talk about purposes in life. If parents don't like their own career choices, it's hard to talk about them. If parents don't know joy in work, they'll need to dig deep and develop a few enjoyable things to share about their path. It's important for them to key in on their job's value to the community. Although material things are motivators, happiness requires more than physical objects. Both children and adults long to matter beyond their "private family community." They want to make a difference in their "outside family community". Parents who discuss this longing make it come alive for their children. The blessed bonus is that sharing such principles allows parents to see that they themselves are indeed valuable, and they still have some choices. By giving children self-worth, they begin to receive it as well. The universe seems to work that way. It won't let us give good things away.

We can inspire ourselves to inspire our children by remembering what caught our interest as a child and what happened to that interest. What would it have meant (or what did it mean) if someone had noticed an interest of ours and provided chances to expand it? Imagine being told as a child to seek joy by discovering your skills and preparing them as gifts for your community.

The individual steps aren't so difficult. They involve playing and imagining. Tiny children thrive on pretend play.

"Now you be the pilot, Daddy, and I'll be the man who fixes the plane."

A seed is sown if Dad replies, "The people on this plane are lucky you're such a good fixer—they'll get home on time tonight."

Notice that play is the useful work of small children. Work with them often. Let them plant flowers and then scout out a nursery whose workers will talk cheerfully about growing things. Let them cook a little and then go to a restaurant where you can see people cooking. Let them get wet washing the car with you, but also take them through the car wash a time or two. You aren't looking for a career for a six-year-old, but it all starts with picturing themselves doing grown-up things.

Around ages nine or ten, monthly career nights might begin—the family could eat out and report on jobs they have "researched." At first, research can be as simple as magazine cut outs or "I can spell 'magician,' and I know what they do." The family might have a career night at home playing games. I've seldom talked to a child who didn't want more family games. You can find them in stores or dream them up: "I am counting little round white things. Who am I?" You can sing songs about careers or make up new ones. Use mime, or draw cartoons, or tell jokes about professions. You know what your kids like—just tie it into careers. The point isn't to become "Thoroughly Educated," like Wogglebug, T. E., in the Oz books. The idea is blending work and enjoyment in the minds of children.

Purpose should be an early part of every life, because "later" gives the illusion of being "too late," even when it isn't. Illusions are so very powerful that they often stop us short of our goals.

If you are intrigued by your work and proud of it, you are a happy being.

IMAGINARY NUMBERS AND PETER PAN

Ergonomics, I've recently learned, means matching products or systems to the needs and comforts of the user. I found a 1920 textbook that filled a child's need for respect and usefulness and even accommodated a child's lesser body strength.

I have a 1920 arithmetic text for seventh and eighth graders. It's small, easy to carry, and its pictures are black and white. It's an exciting book. Here is a sampling of the table of contents.

Forestry and Tree Planting	Farm Problems
Manufacturing Problems	Mercantile Problems
Transportation Problems	Business with Banks
Investing Money	Stocks and Bonds
Running an Automobile	Woodwork
Carpeting	Painting and Plastering
Roofing and Flooring	Heating and Lighting
Insurance	The Family Budget

The book is *Hamilton's Essentials of Arithmetic*, and Samuel Hamilton's preface says: "The problems are all real because they are true to life. They carefully avoid unpractical conditions and all questions that have no common experience." Samuel Hamilton also encouraged students to rewrite problems to reflect changes in the real world—for example, bank interest changes or car depreciation changes. Imagine being challenged at age twelve or thirteen to keep up with economic fluctuations in order to update your arithmetic book as you go! When I was that age, I thought questions and answers were carved in stone. What respect for students!

In 1920, adults apparently expected children to grow up. This little book speaks as if they are future grown-ups. It speaks of careers and personal life competency, ranging from stocks and bonds to laying carpet to calculating time zones. Goals and competencies confer self-respect and dignity.

And the size of the book is not a burden. More respect for the student. Modern texts are huge; no teacher can cover the glut of material in these costly doorstops. No student will ever have the satisfaction of completing a book that big. No pupil will take it home unless forced to do so. Publishers say these big expensive books give teachers choices. Won't somebody please tell them that teachers are specially trained to develop extra resources? College texts are now so enormous that a student spends a fortune on books before graduation. I sense a connection here: money and book size. What a surprise.

Obviously, we're not returning to 1920, and we couldn't because of the vast changes in customs, available careers, and teaching techniques. But we can mine the psychological wisdom in a respectful and useful approach. Why not organize a text to promote careers—math for future programmers, pilots, police, firefighters, pharmacists, weather experts, and astronomers? Honestly, isn't it more interesting to calculate the movements of planets or the measurements and rates of speed for an accident scene rather than deal with a fictitious train race? Today's students start driving at fifteen, and it wouldn't hurt to know about speed and distance, and how these factors can cause or prevent an accident. Becoming competent about world time zones and foreign currencies is even more suitable in today's smaller world than it was in 1920. Finally, let's buy smaller books and trust teachers to supplement. Heaven would be allowing veteran teachers to choose a book to suit their style and their pupils. The 600 page back breakers would disappear.

We need to re-believe in children as future grown-ups. If we don't, they won't. Remember Peter Pan? He didn't want to grow up and do grown-up things. He certainly wouldn't have wanted to know about investing money or planting a forest. All Peter knew was how to fly around seeking fun and adventures. Isn't that just a little too familiar? I think we need Tinker Bell to lead us in a chant: I believe children will grow up, I believe children will . . .

If "i" is the symbol for imaginary number, then why not "i might" as a symbol for imaginary futures?

PRIDE OF EARNERSHIP

Children, like adults, can choose to grow stronger in adversity, or they can choose to grow bitter. Parents can nudge them away from bitterness by providing sympathy but believing they can handle a loss.

One day during my second year at graduate school, I sat on a bench and realized I wasn't earning a cent. Besides the usual exhaustion of reading, writing, and testing, I worked twice a week in a field placement agency and counseled one night on campus at the Marriage and Family Clinic for my practicum. The last time I could recall being so overworked and underpaid, I was in elementary school. "Mom, Dad," I thought, "I did it again—I leaped without looking."

I was ten years old, and the neighbors who hired me were cranky. I knew this, but they were offering me my first paid job. During their two-week vacation, I would be trusted with their flowerbeds. I was proud of the daily sweat of weeding, dead bloom picking, watering, and keeping the soil loose. I was on Cloud Nine when they returned and actually approved the job I had done. But I stopped rejoicing when they gave me fifty cents. I was too timid to complain.

Mom and Dad sympathized and agreed that it was poor pay for the amount of work I'd done, but then, God bless them, they did nothing else. They didn't cheapen my efforts by giving me the money. They didn't make me feel like a fragile weakling by going to war with the neighbors. They didn't make me feel stupid by saying that I should have fixed the price up front.

The "nothing else" they did was a big "something" in my young life. Their sympathy and agreement I needed—it confirmed that I really was short-changed. I now know how wonderful it was that my parents honored me by letting me keep the loss that was rightfully mine. They assumed I could handle the loss and figure out how to avoid another one. I don't know if my parents knew what a gift they gave me; I just thank them for following their instincts.

Of course, none of this had anything to do with my being in graduate school—or did it?

Respect is the most surprising and cherished gift you can give to children—they will strive to live up to it.

NAME-BLAND CLOTHING

Not everything has to become an issue. Some struggles can't be escaped, but others can be squeaked by with a bit of planning and a pinch of restraint.

It's not evil to want brand names. Scads of adults and children want brand names. What people trip over is buying them when they can't afford it. *Zillions*, a consumer magazine for children, researched sneakers for their September/October 1998 issue and reported that the typical sneaker costs about seventy dollars, with popular Air Jordans soaring to $150—so popular they had to release them on a Saturday to keep kids from skipping school to buy them. But not all children insist on brands. Some young *Zillions* readers reported being able to find good shoes for thirty to fifty dollars.

The challenge is getting to know the different personalities that bloom in your house. Almost certainly a topic like expensive sneakers will come up in most families. If budget is important, how does a parent keep from sailing up like a beach kite when asked for $150 sneakers? I think being ready is your best chance. Whatever your personal strategy is going to be, know in advance what you will say as soon as words like Jordache or Air-Jordan drift into your ear canal.

Some parents research compromise products they can discuss with a son or daughter when the vital topic arises. Others prepare a list of ways children can make extra money to meet the spread between the budget and their heart's desire. *Zillions* reports that some parents plan a shopping tour with the child two or three months before school starts. (This is fair. It leaves time to earn any money needed for an upgrade.) Wise parents speak nicely about choices they may disagree with. A boy or girl willing to sweat for Air Jordans deserves to hear, "Those shoes look great on you." Most of us know some adult who overspends on clothes, and we ourselves probably splurge on something now and then. Remembering this helps keep our teeth firmly on our tongue when we see hundred-dollar jeans walking down our very own hallway.

Some families allow children to forego certain family treats and bank the money toward items like designer jeans. I'm not entirely crazy about this idea because it separates the child, but if a family does spend a lot of time together, this strategy may have possibilities. A young person might decide that too many steakhouse dinners, movie tickets, and amusement park trips have disappeared into those sneakers or jeans. Maybe he or she will look at some "name-bland" clothing the next time. If not, then the young person has proved that brand means enough to justify self-denial—a legitimate choice often made by children and adults.

> It's never too soon to learn that an expensive lifestyle should be earned before it's lived.

PUT YOUR MOUTH WHERE YOUR MONEY IS

I saw Sigfried and Roy. They made me believe that elephants and tigers could disappear before my eyes. Chances are, your local lawmakers are talented, just like Sigfried and Roy.

Wouldn't you be so proud? Wouldn't it be more fun than rolling down a grassy hill, if you became one of the sparks that put seat belts on school buses? You've got lots of money to do it with. Your money is downtown in an assortment of buildings called "the government." But your mouth isn't. You need to take it down there.

If a child rides in your car, you must buckle her up. It's the law. In *your* vehicle it's the law. When that same child rides a school bus, the law disappears. Poof! How do we keep ourselves from seeing through stuff like this the very first minute a politician speaks it? I'm searching my house for the machine lawmakers use to turn off my brain.

In 1999, Arizona politicians were claiming a surplus and saying it should go back to taxpayers. Yet only brand new school buses have seat belts. Yes, it's wise to save money, but spending can also be wise. Ideally, our lawmakers could choose when to do which. Instead, we can't afford bus safety, but we do have ornamental iron fences around high schools. They keep no one out; I've actually climbed over one. But they make it easier to catch teens leaving campus early or taking shortcuts. Hmm. Choices *are* values. Administrators care about teens sneaking off, and those fences show it. If they cared that much about child safety, you betcha there would be seat belts on every school bus. You probably know some equally revealing choices made in your town. With your money.

Children don't understand what happens to a body hurtling forward at 30 miles per hour, and they don't foresee that distracting a driver might cause a crash. Many do know that their ride is a noisy nightmare of seat changing, shouting, shoving, and bullying. Until we do get seat belts, why can't we at least eliminate that other safety hazard—driver distraction? Why can't the driver keep parking the bus until everyone stays put and shuts up? I suspect that many schools value being on time more than they value safety or good behavior on the bus. In our hearts we all know the correct moral choice between being on time for class or giving the bus driver time and authority to quell assaultive behaviors on the bus. Chaos interferes with safe driving. Child safety is the primary value. our leaders are modeling poor moral choices.

It is harder for a bus driver to avoid the dangers of driver distraction than it is for parents. We get to drive safely. We can pull into the nearest lot and read a pocket novel until the kids stop being rowdy. "My goodness, is that so? The coach benches you if you're late? Gee, that's too bad—I really wanted to see you play." Bus drivers with a good attitude like this would probably get fired.

Raise the issue of seat belts in your area. Your children will be safer, bullies will be buckled down, and bus drivers will be saner. Best of all, your children will see you standing up for your values.

> *Schools make and enforce child safety rules.*
> *The very same schools transport*
> *the same children without seat belts.*

TRY A NEW TRUE THING

Blaming others is tempting. A creative mother named Sandy showed her daughter how taking responsibility for her actions can help her get ready for an exciting future.

A ten-year-old neighbor named Tina missed a school visit to a farm. She forgot her permission slip and had to remain at the school with a different class. Her mother offered some sympathy and empathy, and she bit back the "shoulds," knowing it would be harder for Tina to brush off a lesson she figured out by herself.

Half the time Sandy's strategy works, but this turned out to be the other half of the time. Two days later, Tina was still trying to peel the blame off herself and stick it on someone else: "Mrs. Connor should have phoned you sooner, before you left the house." And, "Don't you remember? I told you it was Tuesday—why didn't you put it on the calendar and remind me to take the slip?" And, "Why does the principal make us get a permission slip anyway?" Breathtaking! In less than a minute, Tina covered three people who were to blame, and not one of them was named Tina!

"Give me time to think," Sandy said, "before I answer all those questions. This is important." She was tempted to tell her she was blaming everybody in the universe except herself—which was true enough, but Sandy really disliked Tina's attitude and wanted to come up with something better. She considered permission slips and realized that even adults sometimes need them—passports. A passport was a new true thing. There are always layers of true things beneath the first one we think of when children misbehave. (And Tina *was* misbehaving. It's not wrong to forget a permission slip, but it is misbehavior to blame others for what you did.)

Sandy explained that the problem wasn't about Mom, Mrs. Connor or the Principal—it was about Tina becoming a strong woman. She reminded her that every year she was more self-reliant, taking over more of her own tasks. Then Sandy explained passports and said, "When you're a young woman, about to take an exciting trip across the Atlantic Ocean, you won't be a person who has to cancel your trip because you forgot to get your passport on time. It hurt to miss the farm trip, but if I know you, it won't happen again. You have another new strength."

Show children how they create their future selves, strength by strength.

A COAT OF TWO COLORS

Sometimes parents can train children just by being who they are, doing what they do. That's nice. Normally, parents have to work so hard and be so creative.

When I was eleven, I saw a winter coat in Lansburgh's Department Store and decided it was "me." The pattern was small checks of red and black. Mama selected two for me to choose between, and my coat wasn't one of them. I asked her to include it, but for some frivolous reason, like price or quality, it didn't survive her cut. Later, at fifteen, I used my baby-sitting money to buy a red-and-black checked coat. If you set out to create such a moment of triumph for a teen, it would be difficult. I was proud.

Were my parents extra smart or just economical? Probably both. I know they instilled incentive by insisting that whosoever earns the money shall decide how to spend it. This made hard workers out of their four children. Our parents simply spent their money on what *they* decided was affordable and acceptable. And they didn't rush to fill extracurricular needs. I played softball with a sorry, no-padding old glove until I decided to earn a new one, one which I certainly never left behind at a practice field.

Things are seldom exactly as one remembers them. My parents probably would've given me at least part of the money for the glove if I'd asked. My older siblings would say, definitely yes, because they considered me the spoiled one. I should have at least asked. Why did I expect parental ESP in that busy house? But maybe it was best the way it happened — I did take a lot of pride in that new first baseman's mitt and that coat.

Incentives are love gifts, even when they are given inadvertently.

GUNS, JET SKIS, AND HEALTHY HOUSEPLANTS

Children grow character by earning the right to learn new skills. When they qualify, they're proud that you trust them, but even prouder that they trust themselves. If danger is is involved, they are even more entitled to this process.

When did apprenticeship and other forms of training for children disappear from our minds? Children who have never tended to the needs of a houseplant are now given animals to care for—even exotic pets. Why would they know how to do this? Have you ever heard an adult say something divinely sensible like, "Mrs. Jackson has agreed to let you feed and walk Fido for the next two months so we can see about getting you a dog. Isn't that great news?"

Is a child who lobbies to use a parent's "good camera" ever asked to read the instruction book and report back on the care and capabilities of the equipment? Would it really be too much to ask a teen to practice using and caring for the camera *with* the family for a time before taking it out with friends? Apprenticeship isn't cruel; it's empowering. It's a kindness. Even though "just for fun" is an honorable goal for a child or a teen, it matches up with a cheap camera—not your serious equipment.

Lack of training can be downright dangerous. On a beach, notice the children who won't obey the lifeguard, or those who behave aggressively in their waterplay. Then notice that they are frequently given boogie boards with which to assault others. Worse yet, you may meet these same children in other areas of the water on jetskis. Beverly Chandler, the manager of the Lake Mead Marina, says, "The most danger with PWCs (personal water craft) is with young kids. Some of them use them as bump'em cars."

Guns. Hunting is a tradition in some families, and there *are* over-populated animal species, but it's downright chilling to teach children to hunt or even attend a gun safety class *before* they learn to handle anger responsibly. How can we dream of doing this? It's insane to put a rifle in the hands of a ten-year-old who can't pass his brother in the hall without punching him or one who kicks the cat or one who throws objects around her room when crossed. I am astonished that parents do not more frequently connect quick temper to the right to use guns. Let's wake up! No touching a gun before passing the anger test.

The absolute minimum first step in gun safety is rating how well the would-be learner has handled anger at home during the past six months, and teachers should be asked about aggressive behaviors at school. Failing this requirement should mean training won't begin. When children finally do qualify, they should be told that backsliding in anger control will result in a new and gunless six-month opportunity to work on temper control. An angry, gun-toting child is a disaster looming. Once a child earns *any* kind of access to guns, his responsibility for controlling his anger skyrockets: He can't be treated in the same manner as a child who has no access to guns. Mild penalties like grounding, no longer fit his situation. Long-term loss of gun privilege is the only moral, ethical penalty for angry aggression. I'm not open to laid-back views on foresight and firearms. Hindsight is too horrible.

Why not begin at the beginning of things, instead of in the middle?

LOSING THE LOTTERY

*Children are such individuals. There's no sure-fire
way of making them self-sufficient. But we should
realize that it's not an automatic outcome.
We can dream up ways to foster it.*

Suppose you won the lottery, quit your job, and enjoyed monthly checks from the lottery commission. Then, five years later, the phone rings: "So sorry, we made a mistake. You didn't win. You don't have to pay us back, but no more checks will be coming. Happy job hunting!" Some young adults get that phone call. They're used to money appearing quite easily for what they need and also for what they want. There's little connection between anything they do and the money they receive. One day, the merry-go-round will stop, and all the pretty money will get off the painted horses and leave the amusement park. Quite a few young people between eighteen and twenty-one years old experience this shock.

It would be comforting to believe that only children of the rich are getting their backbones softened by too much cash, comforting because we know their parents can keep paying without suffering. But increasingly, parents of average income struggle to provide children with extravagant items and feel selfish or inadequate if they can't. Media feeds these feelings; children and young adults on TV seem to require much and earn little. Ironically, real children are in sore need of something parents can give: training in filling some of their own needs. It's so hard to leave home without this skill. Forget the DVD player—food and shelter may be future issues for an unprepared child. Parents would never impair a child's ability to walk, talk, see, or hear. Often, unintentionally, they damage a child's ability to earn a living.

Greta and Charles are a typical example: good kids of good parents who earn a good living. They get allowances and extra money as needed. Their rooms display expensive possessions. Occasionally, their parents notice that the kids have much but do very little. Sometimes they decide that the kids will pitch in at home as well as earn some of what they want. But everyone is busy, and good intentions fade. Gradually, Greta and Charles stop sharing in the work of the family community. What will happen?

Personalities are clues. Greta's a natural worker. She works for praise or because her interest is caught or because somebody asks her. She'll probably work to support herself. Charles has talents in sports and math. He works for praise or status and gets plenty of both. Later, if praise and status are tougher to get, there might be a gap before he decides to work hard for his own sake. But humans are tough to predict. Maybe Greta will find the transition rocky, and Charles might breeze through it.

Wouldn't it be better if both Greta and Charles had some automatic, built-in work habits? They need a sense of what it feels like to provide for their own needs. Remember, they're only young once. I've heard these words used as an excuse for giving children whatever they want. Actually they are better used as a reason for some wise withholding. Youth is the time when things can be learned with less pain and effort. The chance shouldn't slip by. Scientists know that after you pass ten, it's harder to learn a foreign language—you can still do it, but only with a lot more effort. I suspect that's also true of good habits and self respect.

> *It's a form of unintentional cruelty to give children everything for nothing.*

MODELS-R-US

Look! Somebody's watching us. Somebody very important.
This job is so much harder than I thought it would be!

If we talk with food in our mouth
If we smoke
If we don't
If we brush our teeth carelessly
If we don't mind neatening up a room
If we drink
If we drink too much
If we scream and curse
If we speak well of our friends and neighbors
If we act like mowing a lawn is pretty normal
If we listen
If we dislike learning new things
If we don't mind others sometimes knowing more than we do
If we look at the flowers as we plant them
If anything,

then, chances are, our children will copy us. This is twice as true of toddlers and young children. Teens and adult children sometimes *try* to use us as anti-models: "I'm never going to drink like my Dad does." "I will never yell like Mom." The outcomes of these self-promises vary greatly.

But models we are, and models we will always be. Preaching won't change it. In our "Scissors-Rock-Paper" kind of world, "Doing" beats "Saying" every time. We are models walking down the runway, like it or not.

God whispers to a baby:
"Stay alive by copying big people."

MODELING DRUG BEHAVIORS

*Use or misuse of legal drugs are only variations
on the illegal drug theme children start learning from
peers at ten or so. There are some chilling similarities.
Adults concentrate on differences between 'our' drugs and
'bad' drugs. Will the children do that?*

Everyone already knows that parents who take illegal drugs can't expect sons and daughters not to do that. But many lawful parents need to take a long look at *unintentional* drug modeling that may be influencing children. Careless attitudes about any substance matter more now than ever before. "High" school used to mean higher than eighth grade. Now it often means drugs in the blood stream.

Parents who want to be careful can scan their own conversation at home for sentences like: "What a day—do I need a drink!" or "If she calls me one more time, I'm taking a tranq," or "If I don't get a cigarette soon, I'm going to kill someone," or "Where the hell is the aspirin? That guy gives me a headache that won't quit." These are all common, ordinary speech habits that used to be no big deal—prior to the explosion of the drug culture. Each statement translates to: "Other people make me need these substances." Not a good message to send.

Legal drug use is delicate child-raising territory—strange territory, where what we believe seems not to count at all, while our behaviors count so heavily that it's scary. I remember a childhood game chant: "Heavy, heavy hangs over my poor head." I think most parents are in that position. They are thoughtful and careful about drugs but may not realize they are being challenged to crawl into some uncomfortable corners of their lives. Example: When children see parents get dressed and go out in the middle of the night to get beer or cigarettes, they figure out that the parent isn't really making that decision; the alcohol or tobacco is doing the deciding. They are watching a drug take over and dictate behavior. A child who doesn't figure it out at the time will do so later. Even if the connection is never quite conscious, children have been programmed to be less shocked about seeing a drug cause behavior.

Using legal drugs in an illegal way is even more dangerous. What if a parent drinks too much at a family gathering? Kids hear the tense discussion or angry argument about who drives home. They hear the drinker deny impairment and insist on driving. They hear the sober parent give nervous advice all the way home. The children are scared, but sit quietly in the back seat. They are absorbing. What messages are these two primary, adored role models sending to their children? These parents are saying:

It's okay to indulge yourself at parties.
Just deny that you have overindulged.
Never let anyone else drive—that's admitting it.
Break the law to prove your lie is true.
Risk the lives of the whole family to prove you're sober.
Be nasty to anyone who doubts you are sober.
Stick to your story forever.
If there is an accident, it had nothing to do with drinking.
All the nagging probably caused it.

And

It's okay to ride along with a drunk driver.
It's okay to put your kids in the car with a drunk driver.
No need to call a cab or ask someone else for a ride.
We'll probably make it home safely.
Unthinkable to call the police.
I love you kids, but not enough to risk a huge argument.
Being a coward is the right thing to do.

End of messages.

Not really—they are recorded in the children's heads.

THE MARK AND SAMMY SHOW

Just when parents thought they couldn't stand another minute of their children worshipping heroes with feet of clay, suddenly there came two cavaliers . . .

A couple of years ago, Charles Barkley of the NBA said he didn't want to be a role model. How can you manage that, Sir Charles? Every adult is a model for children. Nature plans it that way. Your modeling responsibilities quintuple if you're famous. The only real choice on your menu is good model/bad model. Serious stuff.

A number of athletes choose the second item on that menu. They seem to find the bad-guy image delicious. They revel in badness. Thus we have the spectacle of Mr. Neon Hair head-butting a ref and a boxer who spends more time in jail than in the ring and can't behave in either place. We see aggressive ice-men who don't know that sticks are for slamming pucks. Fans venerate brutal football players. Are children concluding that if you are famous and make bundles of money, you can abuse others at will?

And physical brutality is only one false face. A nightmare of role models marches through a *Sports Illustrated* article titled "Paternity Ward," the NBA's DNA stats on babies made and denied. One top agent says there are more out-of-wedlock babies than there are players in the league. Another claims he spends more time on paternity claims than he does negotiating contracts for players in basketball and other major sports. What sort of man sprinkles babies around like confetti and then wails about losing a little cash for diapers and strained vegetables?

Kids idolize these crybaby giants. They don't know how lucky they are not to have them for fathers. While real parents try to teach duty, commitment, and purpose, these thugs and deadbeats pose for pictures and sign autographs. How do you explain to a child why a man is not arrested for choking his coach?

Maybe we don't have to. Maybe we have a divine distraction. Something good for kids has finally happened in sports, something that might give them a chance to choose some worthy sports heroes. We caught a break. A miracle occurred in the role-modeling desert—no, make that two miracles. Suddenly two handsome princes appeared, each bearing a magic glass slipper that fits us all. They flash "happily ever after" smiles, and they have golden hearts. They steal your breath away. Disney never scripted it better than:

SAMMY SOSA AND MARK MCGWIRE!

They are princes in all respects. It isn't just the stunning sports prowess—thirty, forty, fifty, not even sixty home runs satisfied either man. Also miraculous was that they refused to cave when relentless reporters wanted them to do battle. Each man insisted he was challenging himself rather than the other and both men meant it. They stayed friendly week after fabulous week. It wasn't some kind of fake public modesty. It goes way back. Each gives credit to early non-famous coaches who labored with them. As a child Mark kept his trophies in the closet. Sammy told reporters that of course he's not number one in Chicago, no one can replace Jordan!

Their magic continues. Unlike greedy stars who will not support their own children until forced, our princes model generosity. Mark gives enormous amounts to a shelter for abused children, and Sammy touched both his wallet and our hearts when he threw himself into the battle to save Hurricane George's victims. And family counselors should keep a picture of Mark in their offices—he's divorced, yes, but still an excellent model. His son not only has the benefit of a loving father living nearby, but Mom and Stepdad are included in the good will. They sometimes play golf together. I'm not making this up.

Gary Smith of *Sports Illustrated* says that the staff didn't sit down to select Sportsman of the Year in 1998. They all knew there would be two Sportsmen of the Year. Makes sense to me.

Once upon a time, in a land called America...

HYDRA

*Mixed emotions make difficult solutions.
There are few challenges greater than sorting out
the threads of an activity that may both
enhance and lessen who our children are.*

Sports are, for me, like the many-headed Hydra of Greek myth except that not all the heads are bad; in fact some are quite wonderful. Unlike Hercules and Iolas, I don't seek to slay the Hydra, and I wonder what those heroes might have done if their monster had been both good and evil. I'm confused. So here's a warning label for this essay: "Take with a grain of salt and mix well with your own convictions."

I don't hate sports. I've played, coached, and spent considerable time in stadiums, gyms and rinks. I've experienced being a fanatic baseball fan from ages eleven through fourteen, and still play golf on the wrong side of mediocre. I've seen youngsters with good coaches (not ego-strutters) grow in character, learn cooperation, industriousness, gracious winning, and gracious losing. With a superb coach, they can also learn how to work fairly and generously with those of both greater and lesser ability than themselves—a life skill they'll need forever. I've seen parents and coaches with realistic expectations form strong bonds with children around sports activities.

But sports can get weird. It's a rare child whose future lies in sports, yet it's no longer rare for a child to experience the pressure of sports on the road almost as if he or she were already a professional athlete. Children of ordinary ability often play on traveling teams that eclipse the needs of other family members. Also notice how practices are increasing and being added onto heavy playing schedules. No time for picnics or science museums or family visits. Sports nuts, big and little, really, really, really want to win—even if winning means sacrificing family relationships. Some of these kids are learning a regrettable lesson, "My needs are more important than the rest of my family's needs."

People howl when you talk like this. It's as if you were taking God's name in vain. Hydra rules. You are told countless (very true) tales about how Georgie was getting into so much trouble before sports saved him or how Suzie went from Ds to As to make sure she stays on the team. I believe in these transformations. But I also believe that Suzie and Georgie would shape up to stay on the team, even if it met twice a week instead of five times. They'd lose more games, but if priorities got straight, losing wouldn't matter very much, and they could rack up some family time. They might even enjoy it.

Television sports affect family time, too. The Game (almost any game) is the drug of choice, and television is the method of delivery. Spouses and children can't speak to an addicted family member except during ads. Eventually, even ad-speaking time is lost as the druggie surfs from channel to channel during breaks. And guess who's coming to dinner. Sportscasters, spoiling your meal with incessant, inane chatter. Dead air is some kind of sin.

What can be done? Nothing easy. In the case of your child's sports, you might have to become a coach or check out some church or YMCA/YWCA/YMHA teams. You might compromise among siblings, instead of letting one child pursue his dreams every year, all year. Or you might let him or her play without you, as in "This year we'll be involved in Scouting activities with Lynn, but next year we'll be coming to your games again." Also, gather some parent power to support good-guy coaches, because the "winning-is-the-only-goal" parents are surely supporting the bad-guy coaches. You might decide that your child will play on a lesser local team rather than the traveling team. If your child is skilled, be ready to withstand pressure from coaches and even other parents. If he or she is really talented, there will be hysteria. You might feel like the holdout on a jury.

None of the above are "shoulds." They simply show that a different mindset is possible. Parents decide for themselves. The only "should" I can think of is to review your own values about whatever your children do. If your morality is violated by actions of adults in charge of your children, you have a right to counteract the unwanted influence. An example might be a coach who claims everybody plays rough and encourages players to throw an elbow, etc. You have a right to forbid your child to do that. Will your kid be caught in the middle? Yes. Absolutely. He or she won't be able to please you both. If the coach won't listen to reason, you have the option of telling your child that you will do the benching if such an important trust is broken.

In the case of the home ruled by televised sports, planning ahead for fun together may lighten the mood. If not, and your partner is sucked into the tube, get the kids and yourself out of there. Plan as if you were a single parent, but invite your mate, even if it's futile. Otherwise, it will feel like anger to everyone involved. Neighbors having the same problem can get together for the zoo or a picnic. It's wise to escape that aura of "nearby but walled off." That feeling can erode intimacy with a mate, and it prevents children from developing any sensible idea of intimacy. Also, continuing to live your own life is appealing—some sports-addicted spouses are even re-attracted to family life and may decide to rejoin you in living more fully in the world.

Sports are here to stay, but so are you. Whether you're dealing with over-aggressive coaches or an unavailable spouse, you'll need all your creativity and courage to achieve a healthy balance—if you decide to battle the Hydra.

The Hydra is a puzzling challenge.
You have to decide which heads to lop off
and which heads to smile back at.

BULL ABOUT BULLIES

People need to hear their own words. With the best of intentions, good people sometimes speak nonsense they would never accept if someone said it to them.

Most of us, out of desperation, have said foolish things to children who tell us about bullies. Every parent dreads to hear that a son or daughter is being bullied. Precisely because parents feel helpless, they look to their culture and come up with bad advice. America values John-Wayne-style "toughing it out," and scoring a triumph over the bad guy. All too often, this is what gets passed on to the next generation. After all, in Disney movies, the bully always gets his comeuppance, doesn't he?

We need imagination and logic to understand how strangely we advise children on the topic of bullying. Let's imagine saying the exact same words to an adult in the same sort of trouble. Picture this: A husband tells his wife that Andy, a big bruiser down the street, has been shoving him, smacking his briefcase, laughing at him, insulting him, and throwing stuff at his car. Quite a scene! Which one of the following replies should the wife make?

1. "You should tell Andrew: 'No, I don't like that. Stop it.' Say this firmly in a strong voice."
2. "You have to stand up for yourself, Honey, or you'll be a target for bullies all your life."
3. "Don't report this. Everyone in the neighborhood will call you a tattletale, and you'll get teased even more."
4. "Gee, Honey, I know you're scared, and I understand why you want to move, but we just can't do that right now."
5. "What did you do to annoy Andrew? You must have done something. He didn't just pick your name out of a hat."

What a difference when we imagine the victim as a spouse instead of a child! The quality of the advice we give is suddenly and painfully obvious. Children are small humans, not little goats or frogs. Their reactions are human and very like our own. They're scared and humiliated, just as we would be.

The next three chapters give suggestions on how to deal with bullies.

Good solutions to big problems are seldom automatic.
Thinking and searching are usually required.
Sometimes we need outside help.

WHAT'S NOT BULL

*Like a magician, a parent can light the area
of the stage a child should focus on.
Rabbits must occasionally come out of hats,
so little ones can begin to handle big problems.*

What's not bull is that bullying happens more often. In our over-big schools, it's easy to avoid adult eyes. A large school population contains more bullies to model bad behavior for each other and provide social acceptance to each other. Semi-official toleration also grows as teachers and principals get overwhelmed trying to handle bullying and their regular jobs, too. There aren't many new approaches Therefore the misinformation of the past lives on, and the odds increase that our children will be bullied or will bully others.

There's no perfect way to help a bullied child, but knowing how your child reacts is one edge, and resisting the "tough it out" theory is another. You can get one more edge by imagining the situation and preparing in advance to support the child. He or she will still feel awful, but the pain and humiliation of being pushed around lessens when the parent focuses on the bully. Children begin to hear their parents when they're sure they're not being blamed. If parents say that the bully has a serious problem and needs help, the child gets a whole new slant. If the parent calls the school and asks in a reasonable way if the bully can get that help, the victim can often start to let go of being a victim. After all, if the bully needs the help, isn't he the weak one? Parent and child might think up some generous replies *in case* the school requires an apology (the school may want bully and victim apart for awhile.) All these moves keep the spotlight on the one who crossed the line. Many bullied children can then calm down and move on to talk about safety tactics.

If your child *is* the bully, then accepting the school's plans to help the child will make a world of difference. Cooperation shows your confidence in his or her ability to change. He or she needs to know that a lot of children have this problem and get over it, and that you will help; in fact, you are determined to help. The next chapter on "Bullyproofing" discusses helping bullies.

*How you see a problem matters to your child
more than you can imagine.*

BULLY-PROOFING, WHY AND HOW

Bullying has been around forever, but that doesn't make it okay. Tolerating it has prevented many victims and bullies from becoming who they intended to be.

No matter what work future grown-ups will choose, they can present no finer credential than a love of learning. It doesn't develop in the presence of bullies. No academic subject is more important than a safe place to learn. The physiology of fear defeats education. Adrenaline suspends body processes not connected to survival. Digestion stops, and you can bet that geometry doesn't make the cut either. Nature has priorities.

Many adults have forgotten how much fear children feel. Fear of bullies operates before, during, and after an attack, and this dreading or remembering calls out adrenaline, too. Even potential victims, who have never been targeted by the bullies, may experience the adrenaline flow and shut down learning—they fear they will be chosen next. A teacher might as well speak gibberish to a pupil in survival mode. The child is barely aware of the teacher. If parents were to keep children "out of school" as much of the time as bullies do, administrators would be incensed about the lost learning time.

The really bad news about bullying is that grown-ups, not children, have to protect the learning atmosphere. Not a popular idea. Busy, overworked adults don't see how they can police bullying. A few sincerely believe children benefit from handling the situation themselves. They're mistaken unless the bully was very mistaken when he picked his victim. When pigs fly and fill the sky, average children will handle bullies and benefit from it. Bullies don't target anyone stronger than they are. The smaller beings lose, and the people they care about seem disappointed in them for losing.

Adult inaction also hurts bullies. They need correction, like a plant needs water. Dedicated bullies are in for a terrible future. Even halfhearted bullies who join in to avoid getting bullied need adult help. They will like themselves less and may start to live up to their lowered self-image. Grown-ups must accept prevention as their task.

The big question is, how can you stop bullies? When I first asked clients in counseling to generate some solutions to any problem, the first answer was usually "I can't—I don't know how." "It doesn't have to be a good answer," I would say, hopefully. Eventually, I learned to reverse the process. I produced the less-than-perfect answers, and as clients dismantled them and told me why they wouldn't work, they began to create their personal, individual solutions. In this spirit, I offer parents, teachers and administrators some less-than-perfect tactics to refute, hoping they'll create some solutions tailored to their situations.

It begins with finding bullies. Perhaps parents and interested retired people could be enlisted to circulate in likely areas of abuse to head off attacks and identify attackers. A "bully-proofing" flyer might appeal for help and warn volunteers that they must treat bullies with respect—anything less would be terrible modeling indeed. If teachers must be recruited to patrol, then administrators should cut them some slack on other duties, maybe even help them with their endless paperwork.

Logical consequences matter. They give clarity. And specific time limits on penalties encourage reform. If the playground is the scene, then x amount of playground time could be forfeited. If misdeeds occur on the way to school, then the bully's parents might be asked to bring the child all the way to the classroom for x number of days. If gym is the scene, then group play might be swapped for a few days of single workouts after school or at recess. Showers are frequent arenas for humiliation, and someone pushing others around there could wait to shower until everyone else is finished—even if it means issuing late passes for a day or two. Learning not to abuse people *is* more important than timeliness, and schools ought to show this value by bending the lesser rule. Lunchroom bullies could sit with volunteer adults instead of pals. Whatever consequences adults choose or create, the aim is to make the costs of bullying crystal clear. Ideally, a bully in rehab could progress from penalties to contributions, such as some patrol time with an adult protecting children in the younger grades.

Most of all, I recommend friendly power. It's awesome. Bullies *know* they're going to give in when penalties arrive at the hands of people who are in relaxed control of their own behavior. An angry tirade is like a storm—it gathers and rages and blows over. Children know they can wait it out. An amiable yet determined adult is a cul de sac, a trap the child can escape only by changing behavior.

Restore the learning places.
Make them safe—they are temples.

A GIRL WHO STOPPED BULLYING

Changing a bully is tricky and individual. You might never get to know exactly what worked. Maybe Nikki's parents picked the right way. Maybe Nikki just scared herself by what she did. Listen to a story told in the voice of a twelve-year-old girl who was there:

Nikki Chapman came from another big city, one that was probably tougher. She had that slightly hard edge in her voice. She was also smart, pretty, and loaded with charisma. Her new seventh grade accepted her at once—she looked like fun. And she was fun, except sometimes she needed to put people down. Joyce annoyed the heck out of her. She was a bit babyish and had long red hair she wore in waist-length braids. Nikki would stand too close to her and say things like "How come you don't shave your legs?" If Joyce didn't answer (she usually didn't) Nikki shoved her. Maybe if Nikki had spread it around, Joyce could have stood it. But Nikki acted like Joyce was stuck in her throat and she had to cough her out.

One day while Nikki was crowding her, Joyce jumped out a window and broke her arm. Everybody swore Nikki didn't touch her. Joyce jumped *before* Nikki could get to the shoving part.

Nikki's parents cancelled her birthday party. They returned all her gifts to the stores. They phoned each person to cancel the party invitation and said nobody was to come by or call or get Nikki a present. They erased her thirteenth birthday. Some thought it was way too much since Nikki didn't mean for Joyce to get hurt. Others said she deserved it because she scared Joyce out that window.

Nikki was out of school for a few days. She came in late one day and got in her seat after class started. The teacher kept looking around and you could tell she was worried about what the class would do. But everybody was okay. They thought Nikki paid her debt. In our eyes, the unthinkable penalty matched the unthinkable deed. If the Chapmans had made excuses for Nikki or given her an easy penalty, it might have been harder for Nikki to square things with the seventh grade.

As for Joyce, Nikki's parents had stamped her injury as super important, and that's how it was seen. Everybody signed Joyce's cast. She turned pink but let us do it. Nikki stopped all the pushing around. Some of us wondered if she was officially twelve or thirteen. Had the Chapmans gotten a year taken off her birth certificate? Who knew how far parents like that would go?

The End

CRUMPLED FLOWER

Some heart wounds simply will not heal. We have to walk on, praying for guidance. We need ways to keep more heart wounds from coming.

Columbine: A plant of the buttercup family, white and blue, state flower of Colorado; any of various plants of the genus Aquilegia characterized by divided leaves and showy flowers of various colors. The inverted flower looks like a group of doves. Of the dove; dovelike. A female character in classic pantomime: sweetheart of the Harlequin, a dovelike girl. So many definitions for the word columbine, but no mention in my dictionary of guns or agony or loss or heart wounds.

I tried to imagine my long-ago high school, the corridors, the bustling, bubbling youth of it. I checked out the faces. Not one I could bear to part with. My mind would not permit imagining even one person just barely grazed by a bullet. There was no teacher my eyes were willing to see standing shaken and stunned by the mayhem. My ears refused to hear any of what would have been heard. Not a single candidate to hold the weapons appeared in my imagination. I am beginning to understand the people who want to raze that building in Littleton, Colorado. This isn't something we know about.

Something wicked has this way come.

THIS ISN'T SOMETHING WE KNOW ABOUT

When we are frightened and no one is certain what to do, we must put our egos in our pockets and weigh all ideas.

We don't know. Our storehouse of experience can't explain children who kill other children and teachers. There's some knowledge about possible future serial killers: Professionals know that children who kill or torture animals need psychiatric help. This behavior could be what criminologists call rehearsal. There's also some research about children who kill parents. But there's little data on our current nightmare: killing in the schools. Later on, studies may help, but people can't wait. They will experiment. In a desert of expertise, people will take steps, and some may be fruitful. I hope we'll be generous and respectful to each other.

Can we stifle our passion to be right and make a truce with ideas not our own? If a beleaguered principal wants metal detectors, if another wants uniforms, if another requires mediation of disputes, and another mandates courses on cultural differences, can't we wish them well and keep track of what happens? I just heard on TV that a Texas principal removed lockers, citing them as the scene of too much misbehavior. Who knows? It might help. The "right" things to do won't be written in the sky.

If parents ask TV to stop airing the worst forms of violence, free speech will survive. Rights aren't absolute—it's illegal to use foul speech in public or stampede people with false cries of fire. Well, perhaps the theater *is* on fire now, and perhaps the industry itself can be persuaded to pass the water buckets. Some CEO's are already studying the types and amounts of violence in their products.

Guns: Closing legal loopholes concerning gun shows and private sales, or setting rules for keeping guns around minors, won't destroy gunowners' rights. Our founding fathers couldn't foresee technology that would so quickly outstrip the brains and morals of manufacturers. Those men were using muskets! How could they guess that multiple rounds could be sprayed into a crowd without the annoyances of reloading or learning how to aim? The signers of our Constitution couldn't imagine that a shooter would be able to kill dozens of people before anyone could stop him. If they'd glimpsed even one bloody schoolyard in our future, those quills would have been flying across that scroll, putting sensible restrictions on gun rights.

Huge schools are a problem. They make some teens feel disconnected. Scientists know crowding is a factor in violence, that peaceful animals become aggressive when crowded, but it's economically sound to gather schoolchildren in one location. Libraries, labs, and sports facilities can serve more students and save building costs. However, psychological costs skyrocket. Teens walk among teenage strangers, and they don't know even half the teachers. They can't feel like a part of the school by representing it on teams and in clubs. Only a few, the very best athletes or debaters, will have these experiences which used to be commonplace.

Also, bad behavior often goes unobserved in large schools. In small high schools, any student fascinated by the dark side has trouble finding peers to share that with. Most have to curb such interests in order to get friends. Mentally ill students stand out more starkly in a small group, and therefore have a chance at earlier treatment. No one can prove that massive schools contributed to recent killings, but people who think so may refuse to let their teens become anonymous in a huge school.

Although parental responsibility must be considered in any search for answers, I believe there are undeserved tooth and claw marks on parents today. Some do need help with serious problems such as alcoholism, drug addiction or violence. Also some parents who are good citizens themselves don't seem to require that good behavior from their children. These situations are admittedly bleak, but lately I'm scenting lynch-think in the wind: "We can't wait for facts. Let's hold parents accountable in court and end this nightmare."

Before we walk too far out on that particular pier, we'd best know that some parents are stumped. Some are even abused by teens and the system fails them. Police respond and sometimes even remove the child—a day or two of peace before release. Parents are told it's against the law to lock the abusive youngster out—just call the police whenever assaulted. I've also known parents who couldn't get an obviously mentally ill teen hospitalized. These situations were not exceptions. And finally, there are parents simply not smart enough to outwit misbehaving teens. Should they be hanged for it?

In Littleton, there's a dispute about whether police followed up tips that the shooters made threats on their website. The boys were not arrested, but that doesn't prove there was no investigation. Unless laws are very different in Colorado, the boys probably couldn't be arrested or even referred to mandatory counseling for making threats. Could the school have expelled anyone on the basis of website threats? I doubt it. Usually, laws don't give much protection from threatened violence.

Parents want to help and should be encouraged to work at what they wish, whether that's lobbying for more useful laws or better mental health facilities or volunteering at schools to see what conditions need improving. Some might want to form church or school groups to fight the worst forms of TV or movie violence. Others may work for safer gun laws or anything else they think will help.

Humans want to do something when they sense danger, especially when leaders have no plan. A wave of children killing children was not expected. Few can ignore it.

Many good people are working on solutions.
Bless them and support them.

SPIRITUALITY

*If we deny the best and most beautiful
part of ourselves, is it surprising that
sadness moves in like an uninvited guest?*

How did we get tongue-tied about the word spirituality? It used to be a given. It was just right there. Now, spirituality is wounded and reported missing. We don't even want to look for it. We pussyfoot unless we know the person we're talking to believes exactly as we do. Not long ago in America, it was okay to talk about different versions of spirituality because we trusted that our basic morals were alike. Who turned off the burner under that melting pot? Don't we know that morality is *still* alike in most spiritual beliefs, and even in non-organized beliefs, and (hang on to your hat) even among most non-believers? Morals are so-o-o useful, and they blend without curdling, so turn the burner on again.

Morals, not church laws, can be taught in public schools. Civil and criminal laws recognize morality. Laws make remedies for bad behavior, ranging all the way from murder to ruining someone's reputation. This alone should make morals teachable. Our country keeps church and state separated. We understand why we can't teach religion in public schools. But no morality? Our founders would be astounded.

Contrary to current views, it would be easy to draw the line between morals and doctrine if teachers were permitted to talk about that line in a routine manner. We all know the difference. For example, a school would be allowed to define charity as good, that giving money, material or service to the poor is good—how much and where to give are decisions for home or church. Even the IRS knows this! Charity's good; it merits a deduction. How much and where is up to the individual.

We have a living conscience, a sacred spirit. We know what's wrong or right. Pupils must find it spooky that teachers are afraid to mention what we all know is there. School is children's work, their duty, where they spend most of their waking hours. Unless morality will be a part of that, I want a moat full of alligators around my house.

I see a bad moon rising. Weird stuff is filling the vacuum we created by ignoring morality. We are saturated with death games and death movies. (A few wouldn't matter, but a tidal wave does.) We have eerie song lyrics—evil deeds are sung of as once we sang of heroism and love. This kind of "dark creativity" occurs when teaching morality and honor disappears. It grows when we fear that our varying forms of spirituality will contaminate each other's children. That's a prejudice with one major difference: it's not condemned. We've bounced from "God is dead" to "God is dangerous." What's next? "God is bad?"

Being mean-spirited about spirit has also arisen in commercial television. Oprah has recently been criticized for changing her daily format to call out to people's spirits. She's a beautiful voice singing in the wilderness. I hope her focus spreads within the media. Joy is native to spirituality. Why should we let all that joy get dusty on the shelf? Open the darn cupboard and bring out the joy!

Recently I've seen another good moon rising. It's called "Going Gonzo." Outfielder Luis Gonzalez and the Arizona Diamondbacks have teamed up with nonprofit Teach For America to nurture some healthy values in hundreds of valley children. Children meet with a TFA teacher for twenty sessions to learn "Gonzo's Ground Rules," such as self-esteem, self-control, respect for others, responsibility for one's actions. After the children master these topics, they go to a Diamondbacks game, meet Luis for photos, get a free Mc Meal and Gonzo T-shirt. Luis has zoomed past role model to teacher. Go, Gonzo! Go, Diamondbacks!

Let's not choose chaos.
Why not choose spirit instead?

THE SQUARE ROOT OF POVERTY IS SEX

*Poverty is not romantic except in novels.
Our babies deserve a chance to get started in life
before they have babies of their own.*

Three people—a boy, a girl, and a baby—will be nine times poorer than they might have been for three reasons: lack of strong ethics, little supervision and, consequently, sex. The arithmetic here is fanciful, but the sociology is stark realism. The boy, the girl and the baby will each be poorer in every conceivable way.

How did teens ever get the idea that babies don't need to be housed, fed, clothed, and doctored? Even the birds of the air are smart enough to build the nest *first*. No one sees a bird carrying an egg in its beak while it looks for sticks. Supporting a baby is a "now" proposition, and unprepared parents without money or jobs can seldom make it on their own. Diplomas quickly become unlikely. Good jobs become something other people have.

Staying together is also unlikely. Odds are, the girl will be a single mom, and if she has no strong outside help, she won't be able to afford rent anywhere except in a high-crime area. Shelter counselors sometimes accompany such moms on apartment hunts. You can't describe the look on the face of a pregnant girl when she sees the grungy, cheerless place where she will bring her precious baby—you'd have to be there. No matter how much she is forewarned, it's a shock.

A financial base isn't the only thing lacking. Some young people don't yet have the emotional wherewithal to raise a child. They believe that babies come on the scene to love *them*. They don't get it that babies need to *be loved*. These teens have it all backwards. It's frightening to hear a high school student talk about a baby as "someone who will love me just the way I am, no matter what."

A colleague recently said to me, "When society stopped supervising and protecting young girls, we forgot that girls, for centuries, were trained for 'their purpose' of pleasing, delighting, and following the lead of their future husbands." These old beliefs are still popular, even in our more egalitarian culture. They're handed on to romantic young women, right along with new messages to study hard, seek your talent, and "By the way, partnerships are now equal." The next magazine a girl picks up will teach her ways to please men—especially sexually.

How smart is it then, to cast unchaperoned girls into a landscape of "future husbands?" Young girls, secretly or openly, believe the boys they love *will* become their future husbands. Is it surprising that they please them by sleeping with them? Is it surprising that they won't even insist on a condom during this sex they shouldn't be having? Above all, they won't believe that their boyfriends are unlikely to marry them. Imagine for a moment that it is your job to tell a girl that the boy she's devoted to is probably not her future mate. The moon hears howling dogs better than she will hear you.

We have to stop leaving teens alone together. Teen girls will try to please and, in the process, will get pregnant. It's a no-brainer. Another sad part of this story is that these girls may awaken too early to a full sexual richness that should have been their future happiness instead of their present dilemma. You hear this when they defend their boyfriends: "Mom blames Tom, but I wanted sex as much as he did." Believing her makes you want to weep for what she's giving up.

This topic always dooms me to days of what I call, "The Crazy Maybe's." Maybe boys and girls should be in separate schools—no, make that separate towns; maybe makeup should require a prescription; maybe horse dates—no cars; maybe only supervised group recreation until twenty-one; maybe no sitcoms that endorse casual sex; maybe that's all sitcoms; maybe put career training into overdrive—start at age 2; maybe sew concealing ruffles on all sexy clothes; maybe hire an interpreter to find out what those songs are saying; maybe mandatory daily sports for all girls.

Only mental and spiritual hard work helps you match up to your teen the germs of truth in your own Crazy Maybe's—which I'm sure you have. Your own ethical framework will support you as you wade with your machete through the underbrush of influences in your child's life, judging which are weakening and which ones your child seems immune to. Your own special prayers sustain you as you make new rules you are willing to enforce.

Early sex is a semi-preventable disease; the vaccine includes spiritual and parental antibodies.

WHERE THE BOYS ARE NOT

Have children lost the need to be lifted in strong arms, or to see themselves in the image of fathers as well as mothers?

In committed relationships—that's where the boys are not. Are we willing to have half our population born outside of marriage? That's scary, even if fathers do decide to commit later, perhaps after several children are born. And many fathers will select new mates when they want a "family." The women who had their babies may also find new mates. Too often, fathers, whether biological or step, move across children's lives like mechanical ducks at a carnival—or fathers don't appear in their lives at all. Think about what your dad meant to you as a child, and then picture that love erased. Money troubles would be reason enough to tremble about no dads, but children see absent dads as rejection, as a commentary on who they are.

No one seriously believes men have nothing important to model for their children. So what has happened? How did boys get confused about sex and commitment? Maybe sons have been forgotten. Parents do seem to worry more about a daughter's sex life and where it will lead her. A girl usually wants to keep the baby, creating a very visible problem, but it's dangerous to ignore what early promiscuity does to young men. Boys need as much help with their new sexuality as girls do.

"I don't worry because my son always uses a condom." First of all, a parent can't know that, and second, it's a sad sort of sexism to decide, "He's okay if he doesn't get caught by AIDS or child support." His life involves so much more than that. Why do we believe that casual, serial sex will do no emotional damage to boys?

When sex is experienced by a boy as "no big deal," and "everybody does it all the time," and "just avoid AIDS and kids," then that young man loses his chance to develop feelings of fidelity and commitment. If there's nothing special about sex, then it's irrational to expect him to be loyal to the one he has it with. He deserves to know ahead of time that trivializing sex may damage his ability to commit and become a good father.

Years ago, I was concerned about China's "one child" law and how people might be affected by having no brothers, sisters, uncles, aunts. I didn't expect my own country to give up fathers. I recently read a *New York Times* article by Elizabeth Rosenthal, telling how China is finally relaxing the one baby law and stopping forced abortions. Ironically, as Chinese families begin to recover normalcy, American families must adjust to doing without fathers!

People argue that there has always been sex without marriage, but they forget that the community used to disapprove of it. This caused men and women to look forward to having an accepted relationship. People also argue that boys have always had an overwhelming drive to obtain sex, but they forget that until recently the community didn't sympathize with their deprivation. The cultural rules made sex difficult to obtain, especially on a regular basis. Sex was viewed as special, special enough to inspire commitment.

Once upon a time, young men envied film stars, musicians, and athletes because of their ready supply of available sex. Most males had to be content with less frequent sex until they married. The movies of that time portrayed uncommitted sex as meaningful and dangerous. Now the media presents sex as casual, the normal thing to do, generally having no important consequence. Babies are paying the price for this. We need spiritual and social CPR. We need fathers. They matter.

It turns out that approving of casual sex is worse than having it.

RHINO

*A modern jungle story shows how universal
is the need for ethical parents.*

In Africa's Kruger Park, rhinos were turning up dead. Naturalists knew the culprits weren't poachers because the horns were intact. CBS aired this story January 20, 1999, on "60 Minutes II." It turns out that young male elephants were the killers. They sought out the rhinos to tease them, stone them and kill them by sitting on them. Unheard of behavior for elephants who are usually very good animal citizens! These young elephants were juvenile delinquents— they had no tattoos and no colors, but they were, nevertheless, gang members.

Experts solved this riddle. What they had was a gang of young elephants raised with no parents to model good behavior for them. The absence of adult supervision also gave them early access to sex, which, the experts said, increased their male hormones and aggressiveness. Excessive hormone production and no family training created a tragic mix. The young elephants turned to crime. I know this story sounds like a family therapist's imagination, but I swear I'm not making it up.

How did this happen? Why were these young elephants left to fend without adults? Years earlier, to combat lethal overcrowding, gamekeepers were forced to move a contingent of young elephants to a different area. They couldn't take adults because, at that time, they had no technology for moving such huge animals in the wilderness. They do now, and that's exactly what they did—they moved adult males into the "gang neighborhood." The big guys straightened the kids out, and the problem is over. The young elephants have been civilized to leave the rhinos alone and wait for sex.

I wish those elephant step-dads could write a book.

MINIATURE PARENTS

*There's a gaping black hole in our school curriculum.
It sucks in little babies and forces them to live
with miniature parents.*

Where to begin? I want a clue, even just a tiny hint about why we think biology, or literature, or math or *any* subject can be more important than raising children who will one day run the world. When teachers look into young faces in a classroom, they know that less than ten percent of these students will make a career of biology or literature or math. About ninety percent of those exact same faces will most certainly have a career in parenting and will enter into that career with zero training.

Biology and literature and math are fine subjects. I really like them. But I would have traded at least half my knowledge in all of them for just a little training in child development and parenting for my husband and me when our babies came along. That is if I had known that any such training existed.

Do curriculum designers believe that this knowledge is entirely instinctive and kicks in during labor? (How does that work for the father?) Instinct may have been enough in prehistoric times when parenting consisted of throwing stones, picking berries, and pulling kids into the cave whenever predators showed up. Sorry folks, but my instinct didn't tell me little goodies like: The ability to lie doesn't arrive until approximately four years old (there's some individual variation.) Younger children don't know that their thoughts are private. They know parents hear what they say, and they don't yet see a big difference between that and knowing what they think. Simple. Makes sense when you hear it. But you have to hear it. I didn't find out until PBS broadcast a science show hosted by Alan Alda.

Think of the implications. A two-year-old who believes you have access to his thoughts might easily throw a tantrum because he believes you know he is miserable and are ignoring him in spite of it. He might have a maddening itch inside his shoe and think you don't care. All the while, a parent may be wondering, "Am I a horrible parent, or does he need to see a neurologist?" I have been told by more than one teen parent, "Sometimes I think she hates me, the way she cries." And she may be talking about a ten-month-old baby.

Parent training in schools wouldn't take so much time. A teeny bit in the lowest grades. Maybe just about the soft spot in babies' heads and about not shaking a baby. Each year another small bite out of the regular curriculum. Ten minutes a day. Then fifteen. Heck, I'd settle for fifteen minutes a week for twelve years. Every boy and girl would graduate with about 120 hours of parenting training! Could we nibble our way toward a fair shake for the babies of this world?

Wouldn't it be lovely if all teens knew how many times a newborn eats in twenty-four hours? And how easily they spit up? And exactly what diapers cost per week? And how often babies have to go to the doctor? Questions like these on high school tests would save a lot of grief and argument between miniature parents. Maybe a few pregnancies would be postponed by such facts. Best of all, every teen would learn about the needs of our most precious product: children.

Sometimes the more sensible an idea is, the harder it is to sell. Why is that?

DEEPWATER HAZARD

Young love is overwhelming, like high waves in a big wind. Parents are the lifeguards, teaching water safety first and then keeping watch from the beach.

Teenage dating can be a hidden reef where careers crash. We know how early sex too soon can alter life plans, but sometimes parents don't notice the ways in which early dating, even without sexual involvement, may affect teen attitudes and ideas about the future. The good news is that parents can be helpful. A parent who knows what's coming can establish advance agreements to prevent complete transfer of teen focus onto dating and away from family and school.

Remembering our own start in the world of dating will cast some light, unless we lived a Disney version—the sweet blossoming of tender young emotions. Rarely, I suppose it happens that way. But more often, fear is what actually blooms, and fear can motivate strange choices. A typical teen mindscript goes something like this: "Somehow I got lucky. It feels so good that everyone knows I'm Chuck's girl (or Laura's boyfriend.) What a relief! I probably won't get so lucky again; I better hold onto this. I better make sure nothing takes this away from me."

In a tempest of hormones, it's truly tough to be confident enough to risk being your own person. Think back and try to remember "that kind of September." It's almost inhuman to expect teens to handle these emotions well. We can't erase adolescent pain, which is okay, because that pain taught us about life. Parents can, however, try to keep the bruises from taking their child out of the game. Most parents already do some protecting. They decide on a good age to start dating; what time to be home; which people are eligible as dates; whether car dates are allowed; whether double dating is required. Parents present the family rules.

But there's an ace in the hole not everyone sees or plays. Parents can insist on unusual agreements *before* dating can begin—this is a time when teens will make bargains. Parents can create some anti-smothering rules to keep dating from becoming the only focus of activity. Before a child reaches the teen years is not too soon to put your attitudes on the table honestly, not hiding your purpose of keeping life balanced. Some possible agreements:

Maintain at least one activity outside the dating relationship; if you must quit that activity, dating stops until you replace it with another.

Roughly one-third of free time may be spent with dates, and phone time counts; the other two-thirds must be given to studies, family, and friends.

No beepers or cell phones because boyfriends and girlfriends use them to discourage freedom and independence. If safety is a concern, parents can get restricted 911 cell phones.

No changing courses or class sections without parental and academic counselor approval. Falling grades mean that you must use the dating third of your time to bring the grades back up.

The boyfriend or girlfriend must be told about these rules.

* * *

When your teen tells you how absolutely insane the rules are, talk about girls and boys suffocating each other with even more rules than parents can dream up. Some require a beeper check every hour! Tell your son or daughter how some teens give up sports, friends, even college, because they fear these things might separate them from the one they love. Admit that when a relationship ends, the pain is amazing, but you consider her (or him) strong enough to handle it. Explain that keeping up other interests makes it easier to be around friends and other classmates who know about the breakup. Teens might even listen if they don't yet have permission to date. Much later, eons perhaps, they might realize that your advance rules were meant to keep them free, not bind them.

Use parental sonar to detect hazards ahead of time; keep your beloved ship on course.

IT NEVER STARTS WITH A PUNCH IN THE JAW

No one plans to be abused. Actually, no one plans to be an abuser. Intentions don't matter. Explanations matter even less. No reason is ever a good one. Both parties must be stopped and sent separately to domestic violence counseling. Really.

Teens trapped in abusive dating don't know it until it's frightful. They ignore early warnings and claim that violence erupted suddenly in an otherwise great relationship. After the shock of the first violence, there's a brief calm, but the abuse creeps back and escalates. Eventually, the police, the hospital or, in some disastrous cases, the coroner will know about the problem they are trying to hide. The main players in advanced abuse learn to blot out the truth about the rising tide of violence. They start believing their own rationalizations and excuses.

Beaten girls say strange things. "It's not violence if I did something he said not to." or "I can't resist pushing his buttons." (Guess who told her that.) "We were just fighting. Everybody argues."

One girl said to me, desperately, "I'm not really hurt that bad."

"But your jaw is wired," I answered, a little desperate myself.

"I have really thin bones," she said.

Parents, believe me on this one—these people will not guard the castle. You are the only reliable defenders.

These girls accept a small, steady progression of control that turns into cruelty. They are in love and functionally blind to their boyfriends' desperate need for control. He takes direction over *two* bodies, and she says that's "caring." The truth is visible to others. Walk around any high school and you see a few couples in trouble. Little invasions of space, small restrictions. See that boy leaning on his hands against the wall with one arm on each side of that girl who looks uncomfortable? He's talking intensely, using his arms as a not-so-subtle cage, so that she has to listen. See that person being pulled, partially unwilling, through a crowd? See that girl yanked or shoved into a car? Listen to the voices. They may be loud or softly angry behind gritted teeth. See that can of Coke so carefully whizzed past a girl's head in the schoolyard? These are warnings of worse to come.

Orders soon begin to take the place of preferences: What to wear, which people to speak to, whether hair can be cut, etc. If orders are ignored, raging begins. Early tirades may include mild shoving or shaking, and the abuser states exactly what "provoked" him to do that. The word "provoked" is his magic charm. It excuses him for acts that may shock him as much as they do her. As his temper becomes increasingly unmanageable, he cares less about explaining himself and might not tell her what "provoked" him. This is when violence seems to come "out of the blue." Until they reach this volatile stage, "provoked" works well, and the girl is fully informed of her sins.

Such a couple is negotiating a dangerous contract. Humans carry "how-far-ometers" to measure what they can get away with. He is driven by fear and jealousy, and his behavior asks, "How far can I go? Is this much all right?" She unconsciously answers, "I don't like this, but if I act right, you'll stop." Step by step, trouble builds.

Frequently, an abused girl tells herself, "I love him. I can't give up this great relationship. Everybody puts up with some stuff." Then one day she looks down at her beeper and realizes it's twenty minutes past her check-in time. Quickly, her shaking fingers press numbers. It never starts with a punch to the jaw, but it can go there. Teens need to know about these dangerous agreements. In advance.

Events like these could already be happening to your daughter. Is she hiding bruises by wearing long sleeves or heavy makeup? Has she stopped wearing bathing suits? Does she concoct tall tales to account for bruises you do spot? She may comb her hair and brush her teeth as if she's angry with herself. She may be furious with herself for setting him off again. Is she very nervous, rather than annoyed, when family members use the phone when she expects a call? Or panicky if her family insists on her attendance at some function? (She probably has to be with him.)

Notice changes in clothing, hairstyle, and make-up, especially changes that make her a little less attractive. Has she dropped good friends lately? She may voice fewer opinions of her own, but quickly tell you her boyfriend's opinions. Has he given her a beeper or cell phone? And have you noticed you hardly ever see him, and she doesn't want you to?

Other signs may be weight loss, dark circles, sleeplessness. Some girls actually shake from nervousness. Is there misery in her face? Falling self esteem and grades? Does she call herself stupid?

Nobody exhibits all these signs, but if you see your child anywhere in this picture, get professional help. Call a domestic violence shelter. They'll have an outpatient clinic or will give you names of counselors who understand this problem. Counseling can help your daughter realize that her boyfriend's wonderful, tearful apologies full of love will come around as regularly as the hands on a clock, every time he hits her—until the clock stops because he no longer feels he needs forgiveness. With hard work, a counselor may lead her to the idea that loving someone does not automatically mean staying with him. Your daughter will also learn that what she accepts for herself now, she will one day be accepting for her children. If the family is asked to come in for counseling, do it. Futures are at stake. Maybe even lives.

You can also call the police. They're better trained now. In most states, you no longer have to press charges—police can assess the physical evidence themselves. This improvement has been a long time coming—it never made sense for the state to charge strangers who assault you but make you do the charging if you know your mugger.

If your son or daughter is not the victim but the abuser, you may not be completely surprised. This teen has probably been at least verbally abusive to you and makes attempts to control you. Aggression leaks out at home. And it's very likely that another present or former family member has anger control problems. Young boys who see domestic abuse promise themselves their lives will be different—there will never be violence. But sadly, in their desire to avoid turmoil, young men often choose ultra control as the method of escaping it. When it fails, they're amazed. They've just slapped the girl they love! They tried so hard to avoid this. It's only a short step to believing, "She's really impossible—no one could keep his temper around her."

Now is the time to face this problem in counseling. Behavior changes are crucial. Save your young guy or girl from a really rotten life. They are on the launching pad. Everything must be A-OK before those rockets fire.

Teach your children to see and reject violence;
teach them that love is not control.
Save them and your grandchildren from bondage.

STAND AND DELIVER

It's not always the teen who has the problem.
A famous example of this occurred in East Los Angeles
in 1981. Some adults who were supposed to be very
smart—smart enough to test the smartness of others—
made problems for eighteen students they
should have crowned with laurel wreaths.

In 1981, eighteen seniors at Garfield High School in East LA broke new ground by taking the prestigious Advanced Placement Calculus Test. No one from Garfield had ever taken the test before. All eighteen passed. With no evidence against them except their success, the people at the testing service accused them of cheating and cancelled their scores.

The people at the testing service had a superstitious belief in a statistical model that said these particular students from this particular location could not have passed honestly. The students' only defense was unacceptable: they had put in a staggering amount of work with a teacher, Jaime Escalante, who respected their abilities and viewed their futures with extreme gravity. He thought their futures were more important than part-time jobs, more important than family obligations, and infinitely more important than "hanging out."

Finally, after much protest, the testing service "allowed" the students to retest. With one day's notice. (This extra bit of unfairness reminds me of one of those Disney movies where the villains stay so excruciatingly in character, meanies to the core.) With only the one day notice, every student passed again.

Other Garfield students were inspired by their success. The next year, thirty-two passed, and in 1985, seventy-eight Garfield students passed the Advanced Placement Calculus Test.

Were those adults at the testing service so out of touch that they couldn't recognize dedication when they saw it? The students who put in long hours of grinding effort threw a monkey wrench into the prejudices of the testing service, and the people there panicked and called them cheats. Incentive and heroic effort had not been allowed for in their probability calculations. Passing the test was a demographic impossibility. If asked, would these adults say straight out that character and effort are unrelated to achievement?

Why did the Garfield students work so hard? Do we, like the testing service, assume they are a wild exception, like that little spot in Montana where some entrepreneurs claim gravity does not work? My guess is that gravity works in both Montana and East LA. When Mr. Escalante took those students seriously, they delivered. Extreme gravity.

The movie about this heroic accomplishment is called Stand and Deliver. See if your rental store can order it. Catch it on TV. Ask your teens to watch with you.

Gravity works—give it a chance!!

HIGH SCHOOL JOURNALIST

Imagination time: Pretend you wrote a letter to the editor stating your opinion that the wife abusers of today might be the child abusers of tomorrow. An offended reader punches you in the jaw. How happy would you be with a cop who gave him a warning ticket and told you, "We've decided not to punish you for the inappropriate letter."

"An outraged football player clobbered a high school journalist in response to an editorial decrying violence." This is the opening line of an article by Rachel Ochoa in the Arizona Republic of January 15, 1999. She tells how a football player walked up to the writer and punched him in the face. She reports that the student journalist had written that "schools have taught kids that they can win by being tough," and "the heroes of today on the football field might be the spouse abusers, drunks, and hamburger flippers of tomorrow."

Some students said the writer brought the assault on himself. Others said that he had a good point but should have "written it differently." The principal said the writing didn't justify the physical response but also said that the author had the "duty to write it appropriately, too." Doesn't it sound a teensy bit like the principal is shifting some blame from the athlete to the writer? Is this a hint that there could exist in this world a good enough reason to walk up to someone's face and do violence? The offender (and when I say offender, I mean the one who writes with his knuckles) received a two-day "in-school" suspension—an interesting but not very frightening concept. The only frightening concept here is "write it differently, write it appropriately."

We are told that the teen's article had been "heavily edited" before it was approved by the editor and the teacher adviser. Looks like the young journalist dotted all his i's and crossed all his t's, which makes one wonder why the principal further commented that he "didn't punish or warn the staff or the writer." Hmmm. Punish or warn them about what? What exactly did he think the staff or the writer did? "Appropriate" is our only clue. It's an overused and abused word, a shield for those who don't want to speak squarely about right or wrong or even make clear what is desired or required. We must guess what the young writer did wrong. Maybe writers must not question the methods of coaches or administrators. (Is their skin really so thin?) Or maybe writers should pretend that there are no future pitfalls for the "be a tough guy" policy that rules so many sports. But reality doesn't pretend—some tough guy athletes do become abusers, drunks, and hold low paid jobs. (Yes, non-athletes often wind up in the same places.) Do those tough guys ever blame their respected role models for telling them "to hit 'em hard—make 'em pay the price." This advice doesn't help much with advancement after graduation, and they <u>might</u> blame their old coaches. The young journalist also said "might." Maybe he forgot to underline it, and that's why the principal missed it.

Some coaches, God bless them and keep them, are strong enough to rely on superior skill to win games—even strong enough to (gasp) lose games. But, do <u>some</u> coaches tell our kids to "hit 'em hard and hurt 'em?" Yes. Do <u>some</u> parents and <u>some</u> administrators back them? Yes. Coaches who are cowards refuse to lose, and believe they *will* lose, unless their players intimidate rival athletes who are more skillful. Come to think of it, this approach is a flat-out admission of inferiority. That's exactly how basketball was ruined: Less skillful players, fearing to lose, turned it into a contact sport.

What's wrong with learning to handle both winning and losing? Isn't that the real way to prepare for life? If you enjoy reading biographies of successful people, you already know about the failures that preceded their successes. Learning to cope with losing is almost a requirement for really big success. Don't let people teach your children that losing is shameful—that attitude paves the way for quitting after a few setbacks, or perhaps grabbing a dead-end job where you can't fail.

Unfortunately, this story ends on a sour note. This story is not success oriented—it is success disoriented. Let me quote the young man himself: "I'm still going to write for the paper. I won't write about issues that jeopardize my safety," he said. Think about that. A journalist who can't write about controversial issues.

A voice is stilled.

CAMEL NOSES

*No doubt about it, children need consequences
when they break rules. But for goodness sake take
time to consider what you want to do.
Children aren't entitled to an answer at the speed of light.
Speed can paint good grown-ups into amazing corners.*

Don't be afraid of camel noses. They're tender. If a camel should attempt to follow his nose into your tent, simply roll up a newspaper and smack that nose. The camel will back out of the tent.

Frankly, I wish camels didn't have noses. Trainloads of creative compromise have rotted on sidings because of the camel-following-its-nose-into-the-tent argument: "Ah, but you cannot grant this ever-so-reasonable concession because then you will have to grant every other concession that is proposed." Not! Anyone in the position of granting concessions is by definition also in the position of not granting them. Choosing is the duty of the powerful. A camel-nose argument comes only from those who shouldn't have power. They're afraid to do a good job because someone might say they were not "fair."

Recently, Arizona schools have had two rather embarrassing camel-nose tussles. One involved a young boy stricken with cancer in his sophomore year of high school. In spite of long and debilitating treatments, he kept up his schoolwork. He was only three credits short when graduation time arrived. Hurrah! Good job! The ultimate in "not whining." This hero didn't ask for a diploma—he just wanted to dress and walk with his classmates. He planned to finish the last three credits in summer school. The school district officials turned him down. But dress and walk he did, after student demonstrations and after he appeared on national television. The rule-crazy school district should have noted the vigor of his battle with a dreadful disease. They were dealing with a warrior.

The second Arizona struggle that went national was with a seventh grader now known as the rocket boy. The boy's father saw *October Sky*, a movie about a boy building a rocket. The father talked enthusiastically to his son about rockets for several days afterward. The boy, not surprisingly, began building a rocket. Not a spectacular one—a potato chip can, paper, Band-Aids, matches, and a few ounces of flammable paint. Along with a pal, he planned to test the rocket after school in a vacant lot. Definitely a mistake without adult supervision. Then he made another mistake. He broke a serious rule: He put the rocket in his locker. He could have received some simple penalty like detention, but he was suspended for a semester of school and had to be home-schooled.

A moderate consequence would not have caused an uproar or attracted national attention. (Is Arizona monitored by hidden cameras?) The overreaction of the school made this young boy famous among space fans. Former astronaut Charlie Walker invited him to a Fourth of July rocket workshop he planned to lead. NASA granted permission for workshop participants to launch their rockets at the Goddard Space Flight Center. The odd thing is, his long suspension turned into a reward beyond a child's dreaming.

Our administrators and school boards have gotten trapped in the jaws of an animal (a camel?) called the "zero tolerance policy." Officials don't see that it's really a zero intelligence policy. Robots could handle a code of rules with a list of penalties to be administered with zero tolerance. Judgment is not required. Ironic, when you realize that most people would say that judgment was a primary qualification for jobs as administrators and board members.

Zero tolerance is surely not a sign of power. It's an admission of weakness: "I'm not capable of making the distinctions necessary to administer this rule wisely." Administrators are selling themselves short. They were hired because they're smart and capable. They can say "no" to a boy short on credits because he was lazy and say "yes" to a cancer patient who worked super hard. They could even find a better penalty for a rocket boy than an entire semester out of school for breaking an important rule. They know the difference between him and an angry boy carrying a grudge.

Consistency is needed, but not consistently. Parents and grandparents know this in their bones. Which of us would require the customary level of behavior from a five-year-old whose dog is sick? Or a teen stood up for her first prom? If we search our memories, we will recall times when we broke a rule, and our parents were wise enough to let us skip our payment to the piper. I received an awesome act of clemency when I was thirteen. I was so grateful that I still haven't rebroken that rule.

Parents and administrators don't need the wisdom of Solomon. They know what's right, and I believe they can figure out how to enforce rules with compassion and common sense if they don't fear the opinions of others. When our own ego traps are pushed away, it's amazing how clearly we can think about a child's best interests. Schools and parents need to consult. They're on the same team. Parents know their children in a special way, and they can help schools create solutions that keep young souls on course.

One of my favorite fictional characters is a little glass cat I met in Frank Baum's Oz books. She trots around so proud of her pretty little pink brains whirring around inside her glass head. I want parents and teachers to have confidence like that.

> *Deciding things is what we do.*
> *Children can't be raised on automatic pilot.*

FIRST-CAR BLUES AND BLACKMAIL

For every rule, there's an exception. I believe parents make the calls. They look at suggestions or create new strategies. So I try to be open minded. But when it comes to teen driving or newborn babies, my brain goes "Phut!" and shuts down. Sorry.

Let's talk about heavy metal and teenagers whisking tons of it across asphalt at the speed of light. For openers, face the fact that these people do not believe in death—especially their own—so don't waste your breath trying to scare them. Get clever. Realize that if the teen's sweat, tears, blisters and body odor have paid for that metal, that teenager will protect that metal. Some teens might even follow a little farther behind the car ahead of them.

Therefore, if you want to be sure your teen lives to become a brand-new little adult, don't buy the car. You don't even float the loan. You don't co-sign. If you have misguided relatives with more money than common sense, don't let them help your fledgling get a car. Threaten to cut them off, refuse phone calls, and send back mail unopened, if they try to "help" your teenager behind your back. Your child's life is at stake here. Therefore, the teenager earns the car.

If you are kind hearted, you will let your children know this before they are twelve, so that they can foresee the part-time jobs and lawn mowers in their futures. If it comes as a surprise, it will be viewed as unreasonable—which it is not. Therefore, talk early and talk nicely about this bomb you intend to drop. Don't put it off. Advance warning may decrease the crying, begging, promising, bargaining, blackmail, and general water torture you will undergo at the hands of your car-wanting child.

In order to fine-tune this car thing, you need to know when you should finally open your wallet. When the teenager has achieved the car, look it over. When you are satisfied that the basics are there and the brakes are especially great, inspect the body carefully. Spring for dings. Buy the paint job the teenager wants. Cool hubs are good. Upholstery repair or seat covers are essential. No cracked windows. Your silent aim is to instill a deep fear of harming this beautiful object. Teens may not fear death, but if the car looks good enough, they may actually get cautious at yellow lights. Especially if they earned the car!

All of us respect what we earn.

ME, TOO

The following fantasy is brought to you today by my belief that parents forget how many services they provide their teenagers beyond the food, clothing, and shelter mandated by law.

You hear about it, you see it on TV, you read it in the papers, but what a shock it is to any parent who hears it firsthand, face to face, from a teen who means it: "I don't have to do what you want anymore." I have a fantasy that a younger teen, or one not yet totally out of control, could be stunned by a parent waiting, all prepared, to smile and say, "Me, too. I don't have to do what you want anymore."

My fantasy parents are quickly alert to a derailment of future hopes and plans. They explain to Paul or Susan how things will occur until he or she decides to reinstate active membership in the family community: "We love you. We'll miss you at the dinner table. Today, I'm buying a small refrigerator for you. We'll put it here on this counter and stock it with fresh fruits and vegetables and whole wheat bread, cans of tuna, and other healthy food you can fix for your meals. We can also schedule a time for you to do your laundry. How about Friday nights? You ought to pack away your dry-clean clothes in dark paper. We'll write a monthly check for your cafeteria bills and explain to the school that while you're on inactive status in the family, we can't possibly give you any cash. We won't ask them to refund skipped lunches. but if the school can't agree to monthly payment, you'll have to pack lunch from your refrigerator. We'll put brown bags in there. The good news is that your medical and dental benefits stay in effect, and we'll drive you to appointments. But no other rides except to second-hand shops when you need clothes or to church if you'd like to go. And, since we aren't in charge of your behavior, we can't sign for your learner's permit during your new lifestyle experiment. Oh yes, there's a box of motel shampoos and lotions on the laundry-room shelf—you're welcome to use those. Can you get a friend to take phone messages for you?"

A family is interactive and interdependent. A small refrigerator costs about $150.

RED ALERT! GENERAL QUARTERS! CODE!

Some moments in life are so hard they are almost too hard. No one can require that you come up with a magic solution. But deep within your soul, you probably require that you try to do that. Win, lose, or draw, trying makes you a hero.

The sad truth is that any addicted child needs a professional, accredited substance abuse program. It's medically and psychologically necessary. Parents can't talk addicts out of using—and if they could, they couldn't detox them or prevent relapse. But sometimes, lucky parents discover drug use very early, before their son or daughter is addicted, perhaps even the very first time. Then, they might save futures.

If your child is caught using drugs and has the nerve to tell you, "All kids drink," or "All kids try stuff," hear sirens instead of words. Stop and consider what you want to do with the next few minutes. Restating your rules is wasted time. The child knows them. Questions rarely get reliable answers at such times because the child expects them and is ready. So you might want to skip them. This will throw the child nicely off balance. Buying time is one wise option. Announce that the family will decide what steps need to be taken and get back to him or her as quickly as possible.

Thank God you still have options. Nothing is foolproof, but many times early experimenters are not yet addicted, and you may have a fair chance to stop them. It depends on many factors, such as which drug is used—you need to check with a drug counselor. But you can also make a family plan.

It should be an astonishing plan. Your child's mouth should drop open when you tell her. Use all your loving knowledge of this particular child to astound her with a big plan. It should be right now and involve all family members. The family system has been shaken, so shake it some more. Overreact. The child should lie awake wide-eyed, knowing that her crazy family is absolutely determined to win this fight. This girl must be jolted into awareness that you refuse to lose your beloved child to drugs.

So how can you make an impression short of kamikaze skywriting? The following are some examples, just to get you in the mood. When you create your plan, remember that if you become unpleasant instead of firm, the child feels justified in taking himself off the hook and focusing on your behavior instead of his own. This happens a lot, and it's maddening. Here are some wild and crazy moves that may or may not help:

1. If you own more than one car, sell one and use the money to pay for substance-abuse counseling. Even if you can afford to keep the car, sell it. The key is the child seeing the lengths to which the family will go to save him or her. The family pitches in by car-pooling, driving each other around and, if necessary, giving up some activities.
2. If any family members drink, even moderately, give it up for a year and all family members, including the child, attend the appropriate AA or NA or Alateen meetings. Make it the new family activity. It can't hurt.
3. A few families turn to home schooling at this point if the child is young and the school is rife with drugs. Some families transfer to private schools which may or may not be drug-free.
4. You might rent a cabin in the mountains for a week, where the whole family walks and talks and plans about drugs until everybody is ready to scream. It's a substitute family vacation that no one will ever forget.
5. You might carry all television sets and stereos and radios up to the attic for three months; the substitute activity would be sitting around the table each evening reading aloud and discussing books on drugs and alcohol, especially life stories on this topic.
6. Some two-income families now drop one income to free up a parent for intense supervision of the child's free time until the crisis is resolved. The graphic lesson for the child is that the family cares more about him than they care about income.
7. I know of one young man who went nowhere without a family member for several months. He saw that he was important enough that both he and his family had to give up a social life until the crisis was past. He's in his thirties now and doesn't use drugs or drink.

Whatever plan you create to show your child that he or she matters incredibly to the family, it should include counseling. Local community service agencies can steer you to counselors with sliding-scale fees, if needed. Also, AA has programs for all family members at no charge.

You may have noticed that astonishing strategies seem to cost you and other family members enormously in money, time, and lifestyle. But any of these plans would be cheap at twice the price. Once the child becomes an addict, you could lose both the child and your financial base. Unless you've already dealt with an addict, you probably don't have a clue as to the costs (in family life, friends, lost education, money, time, heartache, grief, and even personal safety) that you are likely to pay if your son or daughter progresses from sampling to addiction. For instance, how many times do you think your addicted child will help drug buddies rob your house? What little time you may have left, outside of dealing with the addiction, will be spent on your knees, praying.

Face facts. The child has almost certainly done it before. Hardly anyone gets caught the first time. And, so what if it *is* the first time? The child will benefit from the drama of your response anyway. He or she will know how committed you are to stopping the behavior. This is a golden opportunity, like discovering cancer before it spreads. You might save a life. At the very least, your young one will know how much the family cares. If all goes well, he'll be secretly proud of you and use you as an excuse: "I can't do that! My folks are nuts—they'd probably send me to military school or prison if I did that!"

Remember that for you, the parent, it is your first time handling a drug problem. It's probably also your last time because once addiction sets in, you can't handle anything. Then it's up to God, professionals, love, money and hope. A whole lot of each.

Later is too late.

AFTER THE BALL IS OVER

*When you reach your destination you have to step out
of the car; otherwise, what was the point of going there?
On the other hand, if the map was off, and your goal is
a little farther down the road, then continue on.
It makes no sense to go back home when you're so close.*

After the ball is over, it isn't over. You don't get to stop dancing. This can be fun or exhausting. As always, your choice. If your shiny new adult children are self sufficient, your dance will involve learning to dance backward, fitting some of your steps to their new lives. The fanciest step you can do is called "resist advising them." This is tough when you've been Official Adviser for so long, but you'll want to practice this maneuver. Occasionally you might get to do a quick little teaching swirl, but only when asked. Otherwise, you might wind up sitting on the sidelines at the dance, in one of those small, stiff-backed silk chairs.

If you are so fortunate in this life as to have one of these snappy little self-sufficient models, enjoy your triumph, try traveling more, find a second career, and read up on being a good grandparent. But if your new adult child is only partially self sufficient in this expensive, high-tech world, preparing him or her for the future is not quite over. You will need to push through the snags and pitfalls of helping someone who frequently feels ashamed that you are helping. Tricky choreography. You may have to be creative in moral and financial crises awhile longer. Have faith. Minimize collateral damage by planning ahead and negotiating agreements. You can't ground them anymore.

The rhythm is complex, but well worth learning

SHOW ME THE WAY
TO COME HOME

So wise: "Moving back for now may be a good idea. Here's a notebook. Let's negotiate what we both need—then we'll know if it's workable." So dangerous: "Sure, come on over. Bring your stuff. I'm sure we can work it out together."

In a perfect world, young adults would all be self-sufficient. But reality rules, and sometimes the fledgling must return for a time to the nest. If you love love, and if you want to piece together some peace, accomplish this move slo-o-o-wly. You need time to negotiate whatever it is that neither of you can tolerate. Unless you have several mildly uncomfortable but semi-truthful meetings with your potential returner, what you can't tolerate might be each other.

If you are the observant type, you see a glaring flaw in what you just read. Young adults aren't fitted with early warning devices. They want you to think well of them, and they will keep secret their impending financial disaster until their belongings are about to hit the sidewalk. Not a problem. Really. Rent a storage locker or commandeer Aunt Trudy's garage, and invite—no, insist that your son or daughter pack a small suitcase and spend the next two weeks as your guest (no rent, yet) while you negotiate. Your young adult is accepted in the emergency, but not the belongings. If Aunt Trudy can't help out, the money for the storage locker will be some of the best you ever spent. That money can actually buy love. Those possessions, if they are sitting in your house, stress both negotiators. Without that pressure, people who know and love each other can create together a plan that doesn't diminish anyone.

Resentment eats at love. Mothers and fathers will steam when young adults in money trouble buy a stereo or join a gym plan. The parents set the rent extra low so that money could be saved for re-establishment. Right now, they don't care about listening pleasure or flat abs. And guess who will steam about overhearing a parent on the phone with Aunt Trudy: "He sleeps till ten o'clock and says he won't take just any old job. It has to be a good one!"

It's a shame to harm relationships when such issues can be settled in advance. Parents can actually agree to refer friends and relatives to the adult son or daughter rather than giving out public bulletins. Daughters can agree to quit the gym, pay the rent, and save. Sons can negotiate just how good that job has to be, and both sons and daughters can work around the house to pay rent while jobless.

Matters important to anyone are best agreed to and recorded in a notebook before bringing needed items out of storage. Everyone should compromise, but not equally. The returner compromises more. If deal breakers are encountered, the parents get to decide what's okay in the nest they built. If agreement is impossible, then perhaps another relative or a friend of the young adult might step in. If not, there is probably a local Y, and if the parent is able to do so, it would be a loving gesture to continue paying storage for a while.

A stitch ahead of time is a lifeline. Grab it!

COUNTING SHEEP

A strange analogy crept over me while reading a short book, and I recalled a long book, Great Expectations. In this "instant" age, where faster is a synonym for better, is "waiting" becoming obsolete, like our appendix?

Counting sheep is serious to a shepherd. He counts often, and if the count is off, he searches the fields, scanning the sky for vultures as he goes. He hopes to find a healthy sheep lying helpless on its back with legs wiggling in the air. Vultures know that if the sheep doesn't stand up, they will feast. This unfortunate animal is called a cast sheep. (The term made me picture toppled sheep, cast like dice across a meadow.) It seems that sheep enjoy snuggling down in shallow, grassy dips, but if they miscalculate when rising, they can roll and become helpless on their backs. Shepherds have to be good finders and strong enough to wrestle a panicky animal back onto its feet. It isn't easy. I learned all this this from a book called A Shepherd Looks at Psalm 23 by Philip Keller.

Parents rescue young adults these days. It's expected, and it's okay to do that. Almost everyone falters now and then; we've all accepted and given a little help at times. Also, there are adult children who share expenses and space fairly with parents to the benefit of both. But should helping adult children in money trouble be a permanent budget item? People aren't sheep. They shouldn't be stranded on their backs with their legs wiggling in the air simply because they continue to overspend. The instant purchasing habit often brings financial ruin. Do we somehow teach little ones that they should wait for nothing, be happy quickly and always?

If so, change is needed. That shepherd's job is a snap compared to what "parent shepherds" go through rescuing "cast" young adults. It takes longer to get them on their feet, and parents are taking financial risks to do it. The real shepherd is lucky; he doesn't have to pretend he's not rescuing the sheep the whole time he's wrestling it up from the ground. The sheep never resents the help; it never says, "You're my shepherd. You have to help," or "I'm an adult sheep. I make my own decisions."

Self-responsibility for sheep invites disaster.
Self-responsibility for humans avoids it.

FLYING CLAMS AND COLLEGE CREDIT CARDS

*We aren't used to thinking of young adults
as having massive, paralyzing debt.
Who would lend them so much money?*

Too bad both terms in the above title aren't imaginary. They're all too real, if you know "clams" as an old slang term for dollars and "credit cards" as a new term for "everlasting debt." There are now special college applications offered by some very big companies to eighteen-year-olds with no co-signer! Teen-Age Research Unlimited reports that thirty-nine percent of eighteen- and nineteen-year-olds have credit cards in their own names. Chilling. Amazing.

The usual limit is $1000 on these Kiddie-Cards, but some companies simply allow the limit to be exceeded, and charge $25 for doing so. Clothing is probably the most frequent purchase, with music and entertainment right behind—stereos, discs and tapes, televisions and VCRs. Cash advances are also frequent. If you are twenty-one, you can buy booze for a frat party. Some students even charge their weekly groceries. A man I know calls this a "Home Lettuce Loan," paying interest on your vegetables.

Oprah had a great show on college kids and credit cards. Amazing debt totals. One student owed more than $40,000, divided among many cards, plus student loans. She seemed less worried about her future ability to climb out of this pit than did many others who owed less. The students were in all stages of denial and recovery. Some were earnestly working their way out of their excesses, but others simply did not "get it." One young woman, in all seriousness, referred to credit cards as a source of *income!* Maybe if we said "loan cards" instead of credit cards . . .

Some students said it was important to be well dressed. This would make sense if they were ready for the job market. In fact, I recently heard of a wonderful nonprofit agency in New York that is devoted solely to this concept. It furnishes good suits and accessories to poor job applicants, one outfit for job interviews, and a second when a job is landed. The Mervyn's stores and actress Rita Moreno have developed a similar program in California. But all of this is to help people *get* jobs! Why walk around a college campus dressed expensively? Why mortgage the future to appear prosperous years before you are is ready to work? It's a kind of Back to the Future syndrome. Live at your future standard of living while still a student.

> *If, as a student, you live your future lifestyle,*
> *what lifestyle will you live when you are paying it back?*
> *Won't you have to dress well then, too?*
> *Could this go on forever?*

MORE FLYING CLAMS— THE MINI/MAXI TRAP

Young adults can pass a course in finite math or calculus and still have no idea what a minimum payment means in terms of interest. They've never beamed the light into that corner.

On a recent Oprah show about young adult debt, some students said they were proud of making their minimum monthly payments on time. Reality check. The *minimum* is actually the *maximum* out of the student's pocket and into the company's pocket. Alice learned in Wonderland that up is down and down is up, and it seems to be true. Minimums are designed to provide companies with continuing income. They are usually 1/48 of the balance—payments so small that very little money will squeak past the interest and get inside to nibble at the principal.

Pretend your college son charges $500 on a credit card, and his first due date is February 1st. His minimum payment is $11 (1/48 of $500) until his balance falls to $480, and then the minimum drops permanently to $10. (This fixed bottom minimum is so universal that I suspect it's set by law.) If your son makes each minimum payment exactly on time for one year and makes no new purchases, he will, at the end of that year, have a balance of $469.40 left to pay, plus all the interest that will accrue. I hope this will shock him. He borrowed only $500. He will have repaid $127. Only $30.60 went to pay the debt, and a whopping $96.40 went to interest. If he made additional purchases, the arithmetic is even more painful.

How on earth could interest eat a triple bite of all he paid back? Example: One well-known credit card's current yearly interest rate is .1989, charged daily on the unpaid balance—a rate of .0005449 per day. Doesn't that sound tiny? Hah! This itty-bitty number is charged over and over and over (365 times because we are tracking the money for one year) on whatever balance remains of the original amount charged. (If he charges more clothes or entertainment, the daily bite will climb: .0005449 times a bigger daily balance.)

If parents are contributing to college expenses, they might want to explain this arithmetic to their son or daughter. Together they could create a better plan than minimum payments on a credit card. If young adults are not indignant about how much the companies are charging them, ask if you can lend them money under the same rules. If you make the $500 loan to your college student, and he or she repays $127 over a year, can you keep $96.40 of that for your profit? If they say yes, lend them the money. You could sell tickets to the night you tell them you're really keeping the $96. I'd buy a ticket to watch The Wrath of Kahn.

But when the credit card company does the same thing, it's apparently okay. Turn to The Arithmetic of Minimums (Chapter 58) for a table charting each month of that $500 loan for one year. And it is a loan.

> *Credit is such a lovely word.*
> *You deserve credit for this.*
> *I give him a lot of credit for doing that.*
> *It's certainly to her credit.*
>
> *Call them loan cards, please!*

THE ARITHMETIC OF MINIMUMS

First: Divide annual interest rate of .1989 by 365 to get daily interest:

.0005449

Next: Multiply daily interest rate times balance to get the daily interest in actual money:

$.0005449 \times \$500.00 = .2724500$ cents a day
$.0005449 \times 497.45 = .2710605$ cents a day

Then: Multiply the actual daily money for interest times the number of days since the last payment as in the chart below:

	CENTS				INT	BALANCE	PRIN.		NEW BAL
FEB 1	.2724500	×	31 days	=	$8.45	$500.00	-$2.55	=	$497.45
MAR 1	.2710605	×	28	=	7.59	497.45	- 3.42	=	494.04
APR 1	.2692023	×	31	=	8.35	494.04	- 2.65	=	491.39
MAY 1	.2677584	×	30	=	8.03	491.39	- 2.97	=	488.42
JUN 1	.2661400	×	31	=	8.25	488.42	- 2.75	=	485.67
JUL 1	.2646415	×	30	=	7.94	485.67	- 3.06	=	482.61
AUG 1	.2629741	×	31	=	8.15	482.61	- 2.85	=	479.76
SEP 1	.2614212	×	31	=	8.10	479.76	- 1.90	=	477.86
OCT 1	.2693859	×	30	=	7.81	477.86	- 2.19	=	475.67
NOV 1	.2591925	×	31	=	8.03	475.67	- 1.97	=	473.70
DEC 1	.2581191	×	30	=	7.74	473.70	- 2.26	=	471.44
JAN 1	.2568876	×	31	=	7.96	471.44	- 2.04	=	469.40
					INT $96.40		PRIN $30.60		

Total you paid for the year : $127.00

What amount went on principal?   PRIN $30.60

What amount went to interest?   INT $96.40

What is your remaining debt?   BAL $469.40
(If you charged nothing else all year)

These particular numbers are not your friends.

CREDIT CARD PUSHERS: PINOCCHIO REVISITED

Wouldn't you think that we could count on colleges and universities to point students toward success, rather than toward failure and perhaps bankruptcy?

Do you have a son or daughter in college? That college might not be your friend. Remember the bad boys who lured Pinocchio into delights that had nothing to do with schooling? Colleges and universities allow credit-card companies to have booths on campus and stuff flyers in with bookstore purchases. The message is clear: Why wait for the good things in life? Get a credit card, and you will have music and movies and fine clothes, wherever you go! What's this got to do with studying? Studying is supposed to be about the ability to delay gratification, not feed it. Pinocchio learned that the hard way.

Check up on your young adult's college. At the beginning of a semester, go to the college bookstore and see if credit card flyers get stuffed in the bag at checkout. Notice credit-card booths set up on campus. Especially notice whether one company gets exclusive permission to advertise on campus. Does the public have a right to know if colleges are receiving financial incentives for deals with credit card companies? Local reporters should do some digging.

One college had a booth on campus advertising amazingly low interest rates. There was a tiny asterisk after the rate figure. If you allowed that asterisk to lead you to the fine print, you learned that the low rate applies only to balance transfers and is time limited—usually six to nine months. In the adult credit card world, this is a dance step known as the credit card shuffle—keep transferring your balance to new companies to enjoy low rates. Students opening a first account don't have a balance to transfer and therefore do not get the low rate—the one in large print on the sign.

The saddest thing is the change in student attitudes. Having seen the flyers and booths on their own campus, they start to think it's normal to get a credit card years before they have a steady job. They begin to think it's normal to live quite nicely without having any means of support. The financial ruin of students has not yet been fully studied, but it doesn't take a scientific research team to guess that if sizable credit card debt is added to the already heavy load of school tuition loans, disaster is on its way.

Those who can't postpone the rewards of success are far less likely to achieve it.

SIT-COMS AND CASUALTY SEX

An incredibly funny columnist accidentally jolted me into discovering exactly WHO has been pressuring our teens into early and meaningless sex.

Humorist Dave Barry has noticed the sameness of TV sit-coms. He claims there is in LA a computer that spits out sit-com plots for producers: "Three quirky but attractive young people living in an apartment" or "Six quirky but attractive young people living in an apartment" or "Four quirky but attractive young people living in an apartment." Dave sees our mission as locating a hammer first and then locating that computer.

I stopped laughing when I realized the naked (pun intended) truth of Dave's observation and put that together with what these shows say to the teens and young adults who love to watch them. The world is turning before me—am I about to defend soap operas? Help me! Haven't I always believed soaps were terrible training for young minds? Don't they make a girl vulnerable to any unprincipled man crafty enough to hang breathlessly on her words while gazing into her eyes for as long as she wishes to speak? But soaps AT LEAST anguish about sex, as if it were possibly important. And they do acknowledge a rudimentary, if scattered, connection between sex and pregnancy.

The sit-coms don't anguish or connect the dots. They trivialize sex. Everybody does it. Everybody does it all the time. Nobody worries about whether it's right to do it. It's expected. Ho-hum, ho-hum, it's off to sex we go. "Let's see, shall I buy a new toothbrush today, or shall I have sex with one of my friends?" Be happy. Don't fret. No one gets hurt. No one gets a disease. No one gets pregnant. Babies don't get dumped by their dads. No casualties, just jolly fun sex. Just one more accurate picture of life as we know it? Not!

Precisely while I was wondering who in the world would want to promote such inane and insane attitudes, lo and behold, my eye caught a newspaper item. The Writers Guild of America reports that seventy percent of television writers and eighty percent of movie writers are white males, and that writers under thirty have the highest employment. The article cites a thirty-two-year old female writer who pretended to be nineteen and landed a job on a current sit-com. Another writer, Marion Zola, states: "This is the only intellectual profession in which a lack of experience is so highly regarded and so well rewarded."

Light bulb over my head! Bell going ding! It is young males who wish intercourse to become just one more reflex action of the female body. Less than amazing, isn't it?

> *We need to notice who is telling us that only weirdos refuse sex-upon-request.*

A TALE OF THREE CITIES

The natural exuberance of emerging adults often carries them to excess. People understand that. But lately some lines are being crossed too often and too excessively.

| Pullman, WA | East Lansing, MI | Plymouth, N.H |
| Western USA | Central USA | Eastern USA |

On May 2, 1998, in three cities, college parties were brewing and ready to boil over. In Pullman, 200 students rented a house and trashed it, along with nearby cars and stores. In East Lansing, 3,000 students were downtown lighting a bonfire to protest a drinking ban at a favorite spot. In Plymouth, police were trying to contain 500 partying students and getting hit with rocks, bottles, and beer cans. There were injuries. Twenty-three police officers were treated and released after being stoned, and Michigan police had to use tear gas to control the crowd.

These college students are swarming. Bees do it well and humans don't. Add drinking, and we are appalling. The clamor for unrestricted partying is fulminating across the country. Big Fun comes in right behind Constant Fun on the "Things to Do" list for increasing numbers of the young.

We should have seen this coming. Children's birthday parties have escalated to expensive and often spectacular away-from-home events. Cake and ice cream with games afterward hardly exists. The Smithsonian will probably create a display of a small birthday party. High school proms are also painfully overdone and costly. Perhaps even decadent. Can you say "limousine?" Did you know that the expensive tux ought to be coordinated with the expensive gown? Did you know that many teens now rent places to party after the prom? Everything is big. And costly. And crowded. Without meaning to, we've set the scene for these college debacles. Now we have to worry about whether our children will be injured or will injure others.

Humans are not bees. In small gatherings we refresh and test ourselves, finding personal meanings useful for our futures. Beyond the props of electronic games, clowns, limousines, and monster beer bashes, we must rely on our personal selves and the sharing of pastimes to create camaraderie. This is how we find out whom we like and who likes us. We sort and get sorted.

Take your young children on picnics with a few friends. Buy a Ping-Pong table. On a cold day, make cocoa, build a fire, and read L. Frank Baum aloud. Treat your children's friends with warmth and respect. This probably won't prevent eventual swarming, but it may help your children recall where and how they had a better time. They may get beer bashes out of their system sooner—before they are injured or arrested.

Small is beautiful; it helps us create ourselves.

A MEGA-HEADSTART FOR NEWBORNS

Human babies are born too soon. Some scientists say that's our price to pay for big skulls with big brains. Other animals bear infants that develop more quickly and yet they protect newborn fragility more wisely. Nobody told them not to.

Imagine that you are partially paralyzed—you can't control your limbs. the light is too bright, and also your eyes don't seem to focus well. You're dependent on others to keep you clean and feed you. Sometimes food comes right back up or causes pain in the gut. Something's wrong with your ears, too. Sounds that used to be pleasantly muffled are now horribly loud. Footsteps in the hall sound like thunder. You feel as if you've lost some kind of protective shield. On the plus side, you have good feelings about your caretakers, although sometimes they scare you by rushing in without speaking. You don't know who is about to swoop you up at great speed. You're having a rough time.

Your problem is easily diagnosed. You're five days old and human. Dogs and cats protect newborns from bright lights and loud sounds, and they definitely don't permit any snatching up of their babies. Nature wires dogs and cats to protect their babies' brand new neurons while they adjust to all the new stimuli. Their eyelids don't even open, at first. Humans don't have these advantages, and they often ignore the instincts they do have. They press the override button. They tell each other, "Oh, you're being way too fussy."

Give your beloved child's nervous system a mega-headstart. Go slow. Don't take pride in being quick and efficient with newborn babies. Do it all softly and slowly, as if you were just discovering how. Walk slowly, speaking as you come toward the infant. While the baby tries to focus, stand still and talk quiet love-talk before you start doing things to her body. Don't be afraid of offending friends and family with your protective rules. They'll say you're being ridiculous when you won't allow flash bulbs or when you ask them to speak softly. Not giving in will be a beautiful gift to your newborn.

Indirect, softer lights and lower sounds are gifts too. And diapering isn't a conjuring trick. No prizes for speed. Stay soft and slow, and never let anyone bully you into thinking a newborn is trying to manipulate you. Ignore others when they say, "Just let him cry." Take one look at that shaking body, and you'll know how wrong they are. Instinct kicks in when you concentrate on the infant instead of other people. Fathers and mothers must be unshakable, even fierce, if necessary. The newborn stage doesn't last long. Poof, and it's gone! You'll be glad you sided with your baby when it counted.

My sister Margie taught me how to make newborn baths a pleasure. Swaddle the naked baby in a thin blanket, using a three-corner wrap. Lower baby, blanket and all, head cradled in the crook of your arm, into the lukewarm water. As the water temperature becomes comfortable inside the cocoon, gradually uncover the three corners. This avoids all that stiffening and crying many infants suffer during early baths.

If these suggestions sound like overprotective nonsense, recall that imaginary scene of helplessness we set up. The bad news is that it's not imaginary, unless you plan to die young. Fast forward to age ninety-three. Do you want people to let you become oriented, before they start changing your diaper? Do you want them to talk to you while they do it, instead of chatting with a co-worker standing nearby? You'll probably have some hearing loss. Your caretakers should speak slowly and let you watch their lips. You should not be ignored if you cry. In short, your past is also your future, so "Do unto others as you would have done for you." Infants want exactly what you or I would want in that physical situation. If that kind of care isn't overprotective when we're lying helpless at age ninety-three, then it's not overprotective for infants. It's reverent.

I've seen this reverent attitude in action. I've watched a shelter counselor teaching moms to give delicate little back rubs. I remember a mother who brought her newborn to a session, and the way she handled her looked like praying. This kind of loving leaves traces in both parent and baby. They show up as great moments in the hurly-burly that tots put us through: A mom in a park removes shoes, shakes them and gives little feet a massage before slipping the shoes on again. A dad in a grocery store answers a small one's question with respect and a wonderful sort of seriousness. God bless them all for instructing me.

I'm passionate about newborns. That's why this essay comes last, long after toddlers and even after adult children. At this point, I ought to say, "Check it out. See if it suits your style." Instead, I want to insist I've got it right. I want to shout from the back of a snake-oil wagon, promising great things if you'll just buy this one little bottle from me. I really do believe different strategies suit different families, but please let newborns be the exception that proves the rule. I'm right, guys.

I'd like to end by asking a favor. When you're feeling creative with a newborn, and inventing loving strategies like Margie's baby bath, write me. I'd love getting tips from parents of such lucky babies.

Reverence is the right attitude in churches—and nurseries.

POSTSCRIPT TO PARENTS

One day Peninnah Schram, the famous storyteller, professor and writer, came to Phoenix. She told several tales, and one seemed extra special to me. It was about a cold dark night when a young apple tree peered up through the leafless winter branches of the bigger trees. The stars were magnificent, and they seemed to be right on the branches of those big trees. They were so beautiful that, ever after, the little tree longed and prayed to have stars on its branches, in its blossoms, on its fruit—anywhere. Professor Schram cut an apple crosswise and held it up to show us the perfect star in its center. The little tree already had a star in every apple and didn't realize it.

This can happen outside of fairy tales, too. Before a Spanish class one day, a friend heard me mutter: "C is soft before e or i but hard before a, o and u."

She said, "You already know that. You speak English, and we have the same rule."

All I had to do was appreciate what I already knew, but didn't know I knew. I'm sure this happens in situations a lot more important than grammar, and I know I'm not the only one it happens to. I believe there are stars inside parents and these stars can be reached by combining love and imagination.

See the child, be the child,
then let the wisdom of the heart shine out.

INDEX